MW01624767

Coactive Attitude - 7 Attitudes That Will Change Your Life © 2018

Author Stephen Ross

Excerpt from Coactive Living

Cover Design and Illustrations: Stephen Ross

This book is a nonfiction book. The author of this book does not dispense medical advice or prescribe the use of any technique, either directly or indirectly, as a form of treatment for physical, emotional, mental, or spiritual problems without the advice of a Mental health doctor or physician. The author's intent is only to offer you general information in your quest for emotional, physical, and spiritual well-being. In the event you use any of the information in this book, the author and the publisher assume no responsibility for your actions.

Published by Coactive Publishing

Ross, Stephen S., Author

Coactive Attitudes - 7 Attitudes That Will Change Your Life

Description: Non Fiction / Self-development / Faith

Identifiers: Publishing

ISBN- 978-1-7338500-0-1 (Coactive Publishing)

Produced in the United States of America

Coactive Living

1424 E Cherry St. Suite 2 Springfield, Mo 65802

info@coactiveliving.com

www.coactiveliving.com

DEDICATION

To my Lord and Savior, Jesus Christ—To whom all is owed. I praise you, thank you, and love you with all that I am and will ever be.

To my four amazing children—Zachary, Natasha, Rachel, and Isaac. You guys have allowed me to experience love and a better understand of the grace and love of God. I think of each of you as I have journeyed through discovering how to live a coactive life. You have been a large portion of my motivation. I am proud of each of you for not letting the challenges of life keep you down. I love you guys.

To my incredible brother—Dwight, I genuinely appreciate your never-ending support and encouragement. You are the epitome of a man who indeed sacrificed his life for his family. Don't ever think it is not appreciated. You have impacted many more people than you know. Thank you. I love you bro.

ACKNOWLEDGMENTS

There are too many people to individually acknowledge in my journey to discovering how to live a coactive life. I want to acknowledge all my family and friends as well as the doctors and professors that have encouraged me and engaged in the many conversations I have had throughout the different seasons of my life. This journey has indeed been a coactive process that brought about the understanding and concepts of Coactive Living.

Thank you to all who have engaged with me in this process. I love you all.

IN MEMORY OF

Mother - Betty J. Ross

Brother - Gordon L. Ross

Father - Harvey L. Ross

Contents

Prologue

Too many times, people want to make changes in their lives, whether it is relationships, health, finances, or just life in general, only to find that the struggle in changing can become more of a hindrance than the issue they want to change. Often, it is that they are living by a destructive or inaccurate personal narrative.

Our personal narrative is the story we tell about ourselves, which includes circumstances, our character, and our identity. Our personal narrative guides us through life. Another way of looking at it is, our personal narrative is the personification of our beliefs, and part of this is your attitudes. In the following pages, I will be focusing on seven attitudes that will change your life. I should say if you embrace and live by these attitudes, they can significantly impact and change your life for the better.

These seven attitudes come from my book Coactive Living. Therefore, before we begin, I want to introduce to you the coactive living concept. As you read, keep in mind the meaning of "coact." **Coact is to work together with something or someone.** In my book, Coactive Living, I go into much more detail on how and why living a coactive life will better equip you to overcome your issues and achieve your goals. Your life can and will improve as you learn to live a coactive lifestyle.

Think of it as a cooperative action with God, self, others, and life. For example, to cooperate with God—to have a better outcome, one should strive to worship God, pray, and live a faithful and obedient life, as instructed in the Bible.

Living coactively with God will lead us to live cooperatively and peaceably with others, too. In other words, we won't do life alone. However, God is our Father, who has infinite love and grace. You can still coact with God to navigate through life without reading the bible or going to church. A relationship with God does not require either. Although, both will give you a better understanding of who God is and better equip us to coact with Him.

What I hope to achieve in my book Coactive Living is to equip the reader with some insights that will assist them as they navigate through life. My books, workbooks, and ministry will focus on three dimensions of wellness—Relationship, Health, Finance.

To learn more, check out my book Coactive Living.

Three Dimensions of Wellness

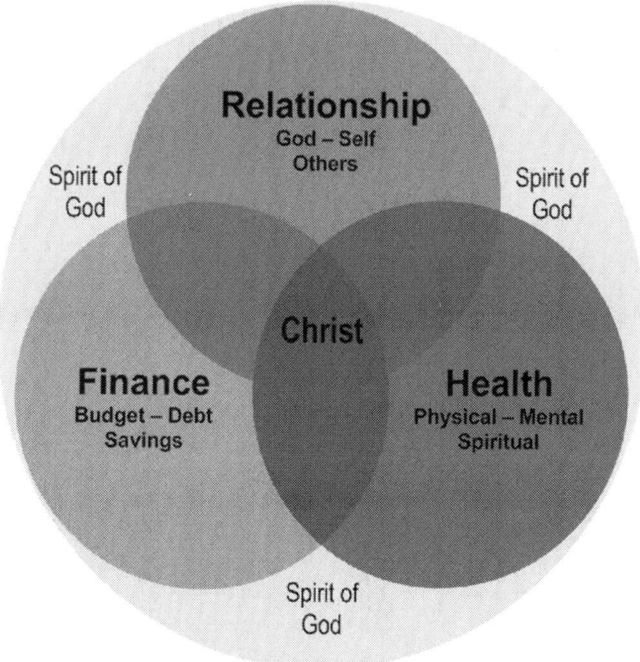

Coactive Living was written to encourage and provide readers with the Psychological and Biblically-based principles that I used to overcome the trials and tribulations in my life. A coactive living approach is a lifestyle that *strengthens individuals by teaching and equipping them to coact with God, self, and others to overcome issues and achieve goals in life.*

The resources used to develop "Coactive Living" are the Bible, Narrative Therapy, CBT (Cognitive Behavioral Therapy), DBT (Dialectic Behavioral Therapy), and ACT (Acceptance Commitment Therapy).

The bible is full of wisdom and instruction on how to live a healthy and prosperous life. The following attitudes in this book, Coactive Attitudes, are directly from God's word. These attitudes are also a significant part of your personal narrative.

In this book, I also want to give you a glimpse at what you will be getting from my book Coactive Living as well as an excerpt from a section in my book titled Coactive Attitudes. As you read, I will point out topics that I cover in more detail in my book Coactive Living.

CHANGE

We must be mindful and intentional to create lasting changes in our lives.

Personal Narrative

Change Your Narrative - Change Your Life

Narrative –

1. a way of presenting or understanding a situation or series of events that reflects and promotes a particular point of view or set of values – **Merriam Webster Dictionary**

Personal Narrative –

1. a way of presenting or understanding a situation or series of events that reflects and promotes a particular point of view or set of values as it relates to one's individual circumstances, character, and identity

> "Man often becomes what he believes himself to be. If I keep on saying to myself that I cannot do a certain thing, it is possible that I may end by really becoming incapable of doing it. On the contrary, if I have the belief that I can do it, I shall surely acquire the capacity to do it even if I may not have it at the beginning." – **Mahatma Gandhi**

Looking back on life, I have come to believe that we have a personal narrative that will guide us through life. The approach you choose to take to overcome your issues and achieve your goals can significantly affect the outcome. In Coactive Living, I discuss the three conventional approaches—proactive, reactive, and inactive. My purpose is to introduce you to the Coactive approach. Your narrative directly influences what approach you take. Change your narrative – change your life! Therefore, allow me to expound on this a little before we go to the seven attitudes.

Narrative

Simply put, your narrative is your story. It's how we construct our events, facts, and beliefs and cognitively weave them together. Michael White and David Epston developed a therapy called Narrative therapy. It is designed to help people navigate through the process of developing their story.

> "Narrative therapy is a method of therapy that separates a person from their problem. It encourages them to rely on their own skills to minimize problems that exist in their lives.

> Throughout life, personal experiences become personal stories. People give these stories meaning, and the stories help shape a person's identity. Narrative therapy uses the power of these stories to help people discover their life purpose. This is often done by assigning the person the role of the "narrator" in their own story." **–goodtherapy.org**

"You or others are not the problem; the problem is the problem."

Your story shapes you and guides you. Your mind controls how you narrate your story. Your mind is influenced by many things—your beliefs, experiences, attitudes, and problems, to name a few. However, your narrative also will influence these things in life, as well. Our narrative establishes our perception of ourselves, other people, situations, and life.

Your narrative about God, yourself, others, and life will determine the kind of life you will live. Again, your narrative will directly affect what you overcome and achieve. How you approach life and deal with your problems will depend on it. For example, in narrative therapy, they teach you that "You are not the problem. The problem is the problem." – **Michael White and David Epston.**

I love this quote because your problems don't define you. You define your problems. The objective is to help you separate yourself from the problem. To externalize your issues rather than internalize. This mindset will help you be more objective when dealing with our problems. I added the word others to the quote because I think the same is correct on how we should view them. Meaning, do not look at others as being the problem. Again, look at the problem as the problem.

Let's say your spouse has a drinking problem that is causing your relationship to be dysfunctional. If you continue to look at "them" as the problem, then the problem becomes personal to them and more difficult to deal with. However, if you separate the problem from the person, you are better able to love them and remain objective about the problem. It may require some tough love, but the problem is the problem. Not the person. Let's say they refuse to cooperate. Now, does this make them the problem? No. It makes their lack of cooperation, the problem. Which should still lead you to make objective decisions in what you think you need to do.

As I talk about narrative, keep in mind, I'm referring to your story or your perspective about yourself, someone, or something. You have many different stories in your life that you narrate. There are many narratives in life, such as political narrative, religious narrative, relational narrative, parental narrative, and so forth. Your past experiences create a narrative. You have a narrative about who you are. You pull from your beliefs to create your narrative.

Both your beliefs and your narrative will guide you and affect your thinking, decision making, and actions. All of which directly determines the experiences you have in life.

Personal Narrative

Your personal narrative is the personification of your beliefs.

Your personal narrative is the personification of your beliefs. It has three components: circumstances, character, and identity. It is the story in which you live out, consciously, or subconsciously. It does evolve and change.

You also have a past, present, and future narrative as well. These different narratives can present challenges as we develop our personal narrative. *We are trying to reconcile who we were and who we want to be with who we are.*

For example, if you are single and looking for a healthy relationship, the process of self reconciliation could create conflict with a potential mate. You might meet someone compatible with who you were in the past, and you feel comfortable and want to move forward in the relationship. However, that person may not be compatible with who you want to be, then as you grow and change, so does incompatibility, and this can cause conflict.

The opposite is true as well, they may be compatible with who you want to be, and this inspires you to move forward with the relationship. Unfortunately, you are not there yet, and that person may not be compatible with where you are currently.

The point is understanding your narrative about your past, present, and future, and communicating this with a potential or current mate is essential in having a healthy relationship. Even if you are married and struggling in your relationship, this is something to consider.

I believe that unmet expectations are the number one cause of failed relationships. Whether it's with a significant other, a parent, or child, a friend, co-worker, or boss; anyone that you are interacting with. Your personal narrative directly impacts what you expect from God, yourself, others, and life.

Therefore, it is essential to know and communicate your expectations. You have expectations that you communicate, and some you don't. You have realistic and unrealistic expectations as well as expectations you don't even know you have. Being intentional in understanding and developing your personal narrative will help you in the process of discovering, developing, and communicating realistic and healthy expectations.

Circumstantial Narrative

Life is forever changing. There are things you have no control over. Also, people in your life come and go. All of which will impact your narrative. Therefore, your narrative is based on certain aspects of your current and past circumstances. For instance, maybe you are a very athletic person. What if you suffer a life-changing injury or illness? The illness will change your narrative regarding your athletic lifestyle. Also, our circumstances vary based on age, careers, marital status, whether we have kids or not, and so forth. This part of your narrative is more fluid than the other two. Life is full of changes.

Also, as you deal with past circumstances, you must keep in mind that your memory is malleable. Meaning sometimes we don't have an accurate account of past experiences. Therefore, dealing with past circumstances should be done prayerfully. They also might require some professional help. Again, your past does significantly influence your narrative.

Character Narrative

Character narrative is the narrative of your individual and distinctive mental and moral qualities. Certain aspects of your character narrative, once you get it right, should never change based on people or circumstances. Some healthy and positive character traits are truthfulness, love, kindness, forgiveness, honesty, and compassion, to name a few. These will help you have healthy relationships. On the other hand, if your character narrative is bitterness and non-trusting, then in your mind, the majority of people will not be trustworthy and could cause you to be apathetic or inpatient toward them.

Our character narrative is what gets us through the tough times, and we do learn and grow in our character based on circumstances, knowledge, and divine intervention. Some people take a little longer than others. I'm mainly referring to myself in that last statement. However, once we establish healthy character traits and are grounded in that character, circumstances, or people should never cause us to deviate. Only grow and move forward. This part of your narrative highly attributes to the process of renewing your mind and spirit. It also helps you overcome your issues and achieve your goals.

Identity Narrative

Many people struggle in really knowing who they are. Having a healthy identity narrative has an enormous impact on your quality of life. If my identity narrative is that I am worthless, then I will live a worthless life. If my identity is that I am fat, lazy, non-lovable, or ________. You fill in the blank. I will live according to this narrative. But if my narrative is that I am a child of God, beautifully and wonderfully made. Then this will be the life that I will love to live.

> "The two most important days in your life are the day you are born, and the day you find out why." **- Mark Twain**

Your identity narrative will change as you discover why you are here—what your purpose is. It also changes as you grow healthier and learn to accept and love yourself better. Your identity is separate from your problems and circumstances in life. How you think of yourself will impact how you interact with others as well as make a difference in overcoming issues and achieving goals in life. When you establish a healthy and strong identity, your circumstances and your problems do not define you. You become better equipped to separate them from who you are and deal with them more objectively.

A God idea is better than a good idea anytime.

I am in control of my narrative. I have the power to consciously change my personal narrative and all other narratives I have. Having the ability to choose is predicated on the fact that we have free will. We have the power to change our narrative. However, I do believe that God is a sovereign God, and He can impede upon our free will at any given moment. When and if He does, it's for our benefit or the benefit of the Kingdom.

Having said this, we must function as if we have free will and the power to make our own choices. We have the ability to initiate thought and respond to suggested thoughts. Whether supernatural or natural, outside forces influence our thoughts. We intern must coact with these thoughts to further develop our ideas, beliefs, and our narrative. I go into much more detail in my book Coactive Living.

When I asked God to change my heart and renew my mind, he intervenes. It's still my free will to ask God, to coact with Him, and allow Him to do so. I continually pray that God will help me change my narrative. There are so many things in life that affect our narrative—how we interpret our story. My experience has developed my narrative. It is my story. We all have a past and a story to tell. You are the narrator. Your mind is interpreting your story and using it to create a narrative that will guide you through life. Besides your past, many other things will impact your life and your beliefs that will continue to influence you as you develop your narrative.

There are rehab clinics, churches, mental health doctors, medical doctors, financial advisors, business consultants, life coaches, personal fitness trainers, wellness coaches, and a plethora of other professionals who are all available to provide a service to help you overcome your issues and achieve your goals. All of which help you define and create your narrative. Unfortunately (or sometimes, fortunately), these resources are not always accessible, affordable, or even sufficient for solving the issue(s) at hand.

Furthermore, many people also turn to any one of the countless self-help books, self-improvement seminars, or motivational speakers—all with their own personal brand or message that promises to deliver. You know what I'm talking about—the books and speakers spouting out words like:

- Just do it!
- No pain…no gain
- If there's a will, there's a way
- Don't take no for an answer
- NO Fear!
- Live in such a way that you always come out on top
- Demand your rights
- Don't settle for anything less than the best

It can become overwhelming and confusing, to say the least, isn't it! Not to mention that, for the most part, many of these philosophies are the opposite of God's will for our lives. They try to create a narrative for your life that can be counterproductive to what God has for you. The other problem is that people (including you and me) have bought into at least one of these lines of thinking. But when we don't get what we thought we would from thinking and living whatever narrative they encourage us to have. Then we start to believe there's something wrong with us.

My message isn't to help someone climb Mount Everest, to complete a triathlon, or to rise to the top in their career. There are many other books, authors, and speakers for that. My message is to help someone change their personal narrative so they can get up out of bed in the morning and joyfully go to work or clean their house. It's a message for the downtrodden and everyday people to have a better life. It's to help people improve their relationships with themselves, others, and God. My message is to help someone look in the mirror and say, hey, I love you. My message is to help someone accept all of themselves just as they are and know that God loves them - regardless.

Before I publish my book Coactive Living, I wanted to do a beta read before I put it on the market. Therefore I gave free copies to a variety of different people with different backgrounds to read and give me some feedback. Some gave feedback, and some didn't.

I gave a handful of books to some incarcerated young men. A young man named Christopher was charged with armed robbery, kidnapping, and a few other charges. After a plea bargain, his sentence was seven years in prison.

He had communicated to me through his father that he really liked my book, and it was helping him. After he read it, he gave it to another inmate. Then I heard the book was making its way through his pod, his cell block. I thought, wow! How cool is that? I felt so blessed by this.

Soon after, his father called me again. He asked me if I could send Christopher another copy because he wanted to reread it. He also gave me three more names of other inmates in different facilities that want to read it. Again, wow! I was humbled and more than honored to accommodate.

Then, a few months later. Christopher's father called me again; he said, "Hold on—someone wants to talk to you." I thought it might have been one of our friends from the past or his wife. But, much to my surprise, it was Christopher. He was on a three-way call from prison. He told me he is getting a lot out of my book.

He said the coactive mind section where it talks about, the emotional mind, the intellectual mind, and the wise mind was helping him. Then we discussed how he was in his emotional mind when he committed the crimes he did. Then he asked me if I could help him get into ministry. He said he wants to be involved in ministry when he gets out. I said absolutely—Ii would be an honor! I told him I would send him some study material to be a minister and prayed for him.

When I hung up, I couldn't stop the tears. God had richly blessed me with this phone call. Not only was I blessed, but God was confirming some things in my life. Helping me further develop my personal narrative to include being an author and a speaker, which is all so foreign to me. I have my times of doubt. Just like you and other people do from time to time — some more than others.

So, what is your narrative? What is your story about God, yourself, others, and life? Where is your story leading you? What story guides you and influences your choices? I can't stress it enough! Yea, I know I'm probably a little redundant about your narrative, but your personal narrative will make all the difference in your life.

Maybe you ask yourself - why can't I overcome my issues and achieve my goals? It worked for 'them,' so why isn't it working for me? In turn, this adds even more frustration to your already often-defeated narrative, sending you even further down the road that can lead to depression and self-deprecation.

But do you see what is happening? You are allowing culture and other people determine how things should or shouldn't be. To influence your mind—your narrative. You have fallen victim to the barrage of ideas from people who are just as lost as you (and I) are. These people are telling you how you should live, what you should look like, how much money you should be making, what kind of automobile and house you should own, and that meeting these standards guarantees happiness.

Then there are also the different theologies, which are just personal interpretations (opinions) of scripture by pastors or well-intended zealous Christians telling you what you should and shouldn't do. It's dizzying! It is also not easy to process everything you hear and read (whether consciously or subconsciously.) Hopefully, testing it in accordance with scripture (1st John 4:1-3 and 1st Corinthians 4:6).

What's more, during the process of processing, at least a portion of what you hear will inevitably settle into your belief system. It will contribute to defining your personal narrative, possibly driving you further down the road of disappointment and failure because you are not able to live up to the prescribed standards or expectations. We fail to overcome and achieve and then wonder, "Is something wrong with me?"

While none of us are perfect, the problem in this situation doesn't lie solely with you. Remember, you are not the problem; others are not the problem. "The problem is the problem." Again, you may be thinking; sometimes, others are the problem. I would say that no, they are not. Their behavior can be the problem, or the lack of willingness to deal with the problem can exacerbate the problem.

> "Trust me. Nobody is as successful as Instagram makes them look, and nobody as pretty as filters make them seem.
> The only healthy and worthwhile comparison is you yesterday vs. you today." - **Dr. Daniel Amen**

In the same way that you are not the problem, but it can be your behavior or narrative. The point is to separate the person from the problem. By doing this, it will create a high level of objectivity and creativity to deal with the problem itself. Furthermore, having the right attitude(s) is also paramount when facing challenges in life as well as dealing with issues. Having a positive attitude and positive thinking is great! However, I think it's more about accurate thinking. It is about having the right attitudes.

When I talk about changing your personal narrative, another way of looking at it from scripture is the renewing of your mind. The following seven attitudes will help you as you go the process of renewing your mind.

> "Do not conform to the pattern of this world, but be transformed by the renewing of your mind. Then you will be able to test and approve what God's will is—his good, pleasing, and perfect will." **Romans 12:2**

> "As we become aware of ourselves as storytellers, we realize we can use our stories to heal and make ourselves whole."
> **– Susan Wittig Albert**

Personal Narrative

We must seek to create an accurate account of our story and live it out in a positive and healthy way.
"You or others are not the problem.
The problem is the problem."

Attitude

Attitude is a Choice

Attitude –

1. a settled way of thinking or feeling about someone or something, typically one that is reflected in a person's behavior.

2. a position of the body proper to or implying an action or mental state.

– Google Dictionary

"Persistence in prayer for someone whom we don't like, however much it goes against the grain to begin with, brings about remarkable change in attitude." **–F.F. Bruce**

Attitude

We can decide what our attitude will be in any and every given situation!

Attitude is a significant part of our personal narrative. It is how we think or feel about something or someone. Often, it influences our behavior—how we act.

Some of the most common synonyms of the word include *view, viewpoint, outlook, perspective, stance, standpoint, position, inclination, temper, orientation, approach, reaction, opinion, ideas, convictions.*

> "You were taught, with regard to your former way of life, to put off your old self, which is being corrupted by its deceitful desires; to be made new in the attitude of your minds; and to put on the new self, created to be like God in true righteousness and holiness." **Ephesians 4:22-24**

Your attitude is also a part of your beliefs and core values. Your attitude, in part, comes from your emotional, intellectual, and wise mind and is influenced by each of them. (Again, this is detailed in my book Coactive Living.)

So why all this talk about attitude? Because you should heighten your awareness of your attitude toward the seven essential coactive character traits. A healthy life-changing narrative requires developing positive, God-based attitudes when it comes to **truth, love, grace, gratitude, humility, acceptance, and perseverance.** If you embrace these attitudes and live by them, **they will change your life!**

As you learn more about how these attitudes are essential for having a coactive narrative, I hope you will come to believe and understand how and why developing the skill of having the right attitude in these and other areas makes life good…better…the best it can be.

Did you notice I said "skill"? You might ask, how or why a belief or way of thinking requires skill? Skill is the ability gained from one's knowledge and practice to do something well. When you consider this fact, it should be evident that your aptitude to regularly put into practice the seven coactive attitudes is just that…skill, or one could say it's intentional.

Intentionality in your thinking will help you in developing your personal narrative and in implementing healthy attitudes in your life.

> "Finally, beloved, whatever is true, whatever is honorable, whatever is just, whatever is pure, whatever is pleasing, whatever is commendable, if there is any excellence and if there is anything worthy of praise, think about these things." **Philippians 4:8**

This passage says to think about these things, and other translations say to dwell on these things. Be intentional in your thinking; fill your minds with good things, especially when it comes to things that are pleasing to God. Here is the way the message says it.

> "Summing it all up, friends, I'd say you'll do best by filling your minds and meditating on things true, noble, reputable, authentic, compelling, gracious—the best, not the worst; the beautiful, not the ugly; things to praise, not things to curse." **Philippians 4:8 MSG**

What we think and how we think matters. Our attitude matters! One of my psychologists said, "You have to get rid of the ANTs in your head, **A**utomatic **N**egative **T**houghts," and I have had to deal with an army of ants.

I want to illustrate the importance of having these seven attitudes by sharing with you my experience in trying to help a friend of mine save his marriage, and even his life. JD and his wife were at a crossroads in their marriage. The stresses and problems had gotten out of hand, and they were on the brink of divorce.

Because I knew first-hand what divorce does to a child's life (both mine due to my parents' divorce and my kids when my wife and I divorced), I wanted to do whatever I could to help this couple put their marriage back on solid ground. My intense desire to help my friends caused me to invest a substantial amount of time in their lives by having them over for dinner and having numerous conversations with JD about God, love, relationships, and what I learned from the failure of my marriage.

Both of them had been married and divorced before marrying each other. JD and Jessica's struggles were common for most blended families, but they also had several other obstacles to deal with on top of those. None the less I was hopeful because I know God is bigger than any problem we encounter.

They couldn't afford professional counseling, and we didn't know how or where to go to get free counseling, so because of my concern for them, I just continued to talk to them and encourage them to hang in there and keep trying. But I wasn't equipped or qualified to counsel either of them. I was still dealing with my divorce and custody issues. As a result, I began to feel emotionally drained when I couldn't see any positive results because of my involvement in their situation. So I asked God to give me a sign if he wanted me to keep trying to help my friends save their marriage.

As I prayed this prayer, I thought about Gideon in the Old Testament. Gideon was chosen by God to lead the Israelites into battle, but like me, he wasn't sure he was the man for the job. Therefore, Gideon asked God for a sign to show him in no uncertain terms that he was the guy God wanted to lead Israel to victory. God gave Gideon the sign he asked for, but Gideon didn't have a lot of confidence in himself (or God, so it seems), so he asked God again for another sign. And again, God gave Gideon precisely what he asked. Gideon was finally convinced. He did indeed lead Israel in one of the most incredible battles and victories in history.

The signs Gideon asked for involved sheep fleece. I wasn't into sheep fleece, though, so I asked God to give me a pure silver coin if he wanted me to continue helping my friends try to salvage their marriage.

Since I worked in retail, I thought it was a reasonable request to ask for a pure silver coin since it wasn't too unusual for me to come across one in the cash register. I thought pure silver coins were pretty cool, so whenever I did find one, I would buy it out of the cash register. However, during this time, I was managing a different type of establishment, we did not get change (coins) very much, and I hadn't seen a pure silver coin for quite some time. So I thought that would be a way for me to recognize if this was something God wanted me to do.

For the next three or four weeks, I looked for a silver coin every day. I got nothing. I dismissed my request and continued to minister to JD anyway. During that time, JD's wife left the marriage with no intention or desire to come back. I did, however, continue to talk to JD and encourage him to stay strong and focus on being a great dad to his kids.

A week or so later, I answered the phone and heard, "Teach my kids about God, Steve t-t-teach my kids about God!" he cried out. JD was out of control and was mercilessly crying. My heart dropped to my stomach as I felt his desperation. I heard the hopelessness in his voice. I implored. "Calm down, JD. Calm down." JD desperately replied. "No! You don't understand! Just teach my kids about God."

He hung up the phone. I immediately looked at my caller ID and called him back. There was no answer. I knew that the number was not his phone number. He had called from a payphone, so I had no idea where he was.

A year prior, another friend of mine, Bret, also wanted to end his life. He shot himself in the head with a nail gun, placing a three-inch nail into his brain. Miraculously, God intervened, and he survived. This previous experience caused me to be even more worried about JD. I go into more detail about my experience with Bret in my book Coactive Living.

Again, God intervened in JD's situation and connected me with a Christian policeman and a caring 9-1-1 operator who helped me track him down before it was too late. The officer called me back a few hours after my 9-1-1 call and told me that he found JD unconscious in his car with a hose running from the exhaust. They revived him, and he is in the hospital recovering.

When I got to the hospital, JD was a little groggy, but he was doing just fine. He said he knew I was praying for him because when he tried the first time, the hose melted, and then it wasn't long enough. So, he had to go to K-mart and by another hose. We both laughed and thanked God he was still alive.

Upon his release from the hospital, JD was admitted to a mental health ward for three days for a formal evaluation. I went to visit him several times and ministered to him the best I knew how. Only a few days after his release, he 'lost it' again when he discovered his soon-to-be ex-wife was with another man in a hotel room.

The next hour or so was like something you'd see on television. Not wanting JD to hurt (or kill) himself and someone else, I convinced him to tell me where his wife and her 'friend' were at and insisted that he stay home. When I got there, I knocked on the door. She let me in, telling me her friend had just left because JD had vandalized her car. She then added that she had called the police because he was going after her friend.

As I drove home, I prayed, asking God what to do next. Shortly after I got home, a police officer had called me. I stepped outside my apartment so that my kids could not hear. The officer explained about a struggle over a gun between JD and the other man, but thankfully no one was hurt. They were searching for JD, though, because he was an unstable man with a gun on the loose, and no one had a clue as to what he might do next.

As I hung up the phone, I looked down at the ground, and something shiny caught my eye. I reached down to pick it up. It was a dime. But not just any ordinary dime. It was a pure silver 1945 mercury dime. It was my sign from God!

Feeling weak all over, I went back inside, plopped down in a chair, and looked at the dime feeling both flabbergasted and excited all together. After a minute or so, I started uncontrollably laughing and crying at the same time.

"God," I said, "You are an incomprehensible God. Thank you. Thank you, Lord. Thank you."

In that instant, I also realized there was no reason for me to worry about JD any longer. He was in God's hands—the very best place any of us can be. I did, however, start praying for him right then and there.

"Lord, please let JD call me and tell me he knows he will be okay. Oh, and Lord, when he does give me the words to say back to him."

You know what happened next, don't you? That's right—not too long after the prayer, the phone rang. It was JD telling me what had taken place. I encouraged him to turn himself in and trust the Lord to watch over him. He was resistant at first. He didn't want to go to jail. Who would? But after talking with him for a while, he took a step of faith and turned himself in.

This leap of faith paid off for JD in a big way. He didn't go to jail. There were not even any charges brought against him.

The whole experience taught him a lot about faith and was a real turning point in his relationship with God. I know it sure brought me closer to God.

Fast-forward several years. I had been invited to speak at a church and was planning to use this incident as part of my sermon. As I was preparing for the event, I finally decided to ask JD the question I'd wanted to ask him since that night. "When you took the gun, why didn't you shoot him? Or kill yourself?"

His reply: "I tried. The gun wasn't loaded."

Thank God for that!

So as we venture through the following attitudes, I will refer to this story to help illustrate the seven life-changing attitudes. I hope to illustrate the difference between having these attitudes and not.

> "Again and again, God's Word reveals that He is not as concerned about the depth or extent of the sin we commit as He is about our attitude and response when we are confronted with our sin." - **Nancy Leigh DeMoss**

Attitude

"The longer I live, the more I realize the impact of attitude on life. Attitude, to me, is more important than facts. It is more important than the past, than education, than money, than circumstances, than failures, than successes, than what other people think or say or do. It is more important than appearance, giftedness, or skill. It will make or break a company ... a church ... a home. The remarkable thing is we have a choice every day regarding the attitude we will embrace for that day. We cannot change the inevitable. The only thing we can do is play on the one string we have, and that is our attitude ... I am convinced that life is 10% what happens to me, and 90% how I react to it. And so, it is with you ... we are in charge of our Attitudes." ~ **Charles Swindoll.**

ATTITUDE

We must have the right attitudes

to live a healthy and joyful life.

Attitude 1

Attitude of Truth

Truth –

1. The quality of being true

True –

1. In accordance with fact or reality.
2. Accurate or exact.
3. Loyal or faithful.
4. Honest.

Dictionary.com

"Truth will always be truth, regardless of lack of understanding, disbelief or ignorance." **– W. Clement Stone**

The pursuit of truth is a lifelong endeavor. To some, truth is absolute, while to others, it's relative to their reality. Truth is filtered through our perception, which is the reality in which most people live. In other words, our personal narrative.

But to have a genuine attitude of truth, one must step out of their current personal narrative and be open to other possibilities. Walking in truth enlightens our path and mitigates faulty thinking. We must be willing to accept the fact that my personal narrative, my beliefs can be flawed and wrong.

Some people would say that there is no such thing as ABSOLUTE TRUTH. But I disagree. I believe there are absolute truths because I believe in the sovereignty of God. I also think that there are truths that are a matter of perspective. There can be two truths that contradict each other. And both be true. Take a good look at the following picture.

So, what do you see in the picture? A duck or a rabbit? Or both? In this case, the truth is relative. A few examples of absolute truth is, there are no round squares, and the earth is spherical. People that argue against absolute truths will attempt to redefine both of these examples by changing the context.

Context is required when pursuing truth, whether it is absolute or relative. However, some may argue that if the context is necessary, then it's not absolute. Anyway, let's not go down the rabbit trail of philosophical arguments about absolute truth. I just wanted to challenge some people's thinking.

Let me present it this way; the thing about truth is it can be relative or absolute in a point of time. Some truth is altered or changed depending on the vantage point, or circumstances, i.e., the rabbit or duck picture. Other truths remain the same no matter what vantage point or circumstances it is subjected to in a point of time. Two opposite views have caused many arguments that have ruined families and friendships.

Here is what matters. The thing about having an attitude of truth is you desire and choose to pursue truth and consider all options. Finding the truth is more important than winning the argument. If you don't have this attitude as a part of your personal narrative, then you will get lost in semantics or dogma, and both can rob you of the peace in life.

The difficulty with the truth, however, is that Satan, people, or cultural influences can often deceive you and trick you into accepting lies as truth. This deception can cause you to live with flawed thinking and faulty narratives and beliefs.

For example, just because people believe that there is no God, does not make it true. The opposite is correct as well, just because I believe God is real does not make it so. In this case, one's truth is a matter of perspective. Or is it? No matter one's perspective, the facts are the facts whether we accept them or not. In this example, our understanding of truth becomes a decision.

The decision to accept the truth is, for all practical purposes, faith. What you accept as truth is a decision. I accept God's word as truth.

His word (the bible) is a truth that I live by and prayerfully pursue. Even though God's word is true, my interpretation of his word may not represent the truth. Therefore I must continue to seek God's revelation of the truth.

As far as faith, it's not only about the 'God kind' of faith. I'm also talking about faith in general. Yes, I have faith that God is real and actively present in my life. But I also have faith in many other areas of life. For example, every time I stop at a traffic light, it is going to turn green so I can continue on my way.

In the case of JD, his truth was that he was not valuable enough to live. His truth was that he would be better off dead. My truth, on the other hand, was that he was valuable to his kids as their father, to me as his friend, and to God as his child. Those truths caused me to believe that he was valuable enough to live.

Now let's go back to the night he tried to commit suicide in his car. That night JD's truth was nothing more than a false personal narrative or rather a lie from Satan. However, his narrative changed when he was saved, and his life was spared. At that point, his truth was God saved him because he loves him.

Another perspective of what truth is in that situation comes from the police officer that rescued JD from his car. The officer told me he was a Christian and that he felt led into the alley to the car that night by the Holy Spirit. His truth is that God used him to intervene in a desperate man's life to help save it.

The ultimate truth, however, comes from God the Father and Jesus, the son. We see this clearly and undeniably when Jesus said,

> "If you hold to my teaching, you are really my disciples. Then you will know the truth, and the truth will set you free." **John 8:31-32**

The truth Jesus is talking about here can be found in the Gospel of Matthew.

> "Jesus replied: "'Love the Lord your God with all your heart and with all your soul and with all your mind.' This is the first and greatest commandment. And the second is like it: 'Love your neighbor as yourself.' All the Law and the Prophets hang on these two commandments." **Matthew 22:37-40**

Jesus' teaching here is to Love God with all that I am—to love myself and to love others. This is a truth we are called to live by. It is the truth that gives me much freedom and joy. It is also the truth that is centered around other truths I hold—specifically the truth that God is as real as the air we breathe, and that the Bible offers us great wisdom on how to live our lives.

Having an attitude of truth indicates that we will mindfully search for truth in what we believe, in what we see and hear, and in our circumstances. This attitude of truth should cause us to present ourselves with integrity.

During my adolescent years and even into my early adult years, I did not have an attitude of truth. Lying was second nature to me—especially when I wanted something or wished to avoid conflict. It was a pattern of behavior I developed as a result of living those years in 'survivor mode.' My childhood was like a modern-day version of Huckleberry Finn. It was also a pattern of behavior that proved to be fatally destructive to my marriage, as well as several other aspects of my life.

When I was in my mid twenty's God delivered me from the toxic attitude of lying and instilled in me a desire to have an attitude of truth. During this time, I made a commitment to God and myself. The commitment was this: every time I realized I was lying, I would immediately admit the lie to the person I was speaking to and asked for forgiveness.

For the most part, I did stick to this commitment. It wasn't easy. It was embarrassing and humbling, but God honored my commitment and renewed my mind in this area of my life. Even to this day, I do my very best to honor this commitment. My personal narrative regarding truth changed. Therefore, I changed.

An attitude of truth causes you to pursue truth and live a truthful life. Truth is essential for living a coactive life. Furthermore, I cannot stress enough that having an attitude of truth will bring enormous peace and harmony to your life. There is no darkness in truth. Untruths bring stress to your life. Think about it—if you do not know the truth – how can you deal with it?

Truth is also essential for healthy relationships. Relationships are built on genuineness rather than falsehoods and unrealistic expectations when we know the truth about the people we have relationships with, and they know the truth about us.

Having an attitude of truth as an essential part of your personal narrative. It will allow you to be open to, and accepting truths about God, ourselves, others, and life. It will bring you peace and grow you and your relationships. We need people in our life that we can be authentic with, especially our significant other. Furthermore, love speaks the truth, and when you speak or receive truth from a heart of love, rejoice in it. Truth indeed is the way to live with God the Father and Jesus, the son.

> "Our heavenly Father understands our disappointment, suffering, pain, fear, and doubt. He is always there to encourage our hearts and help us understand that He's sufficient for all of our needs. When I accepted this as an absolute truth in my life, I found that my worrying stopped." – **Charles Stanley**

TRUTH

We must seek it, find it, and live it!

Live it through our thoughts, our words, and our actions.

Attitude 2

Attitude of Love

Love –

1. A profoundly tender, passionate affection for another person.
2. A feeling of warm personal attachment or deep affection
3. Sexual passion or desire.

Dictionary.com

> "To love you as I should, I must worship God as Creator. When I have learnt to love God better than my earthly dearest, I shall love my earthly dearest better than I do now. In so far as I learn to love my earthly dearest at the expense of God and instead of God, I shall be moving towards the state in which I shall not love my earthly dearest at all. When first things are put first, second things are not suppressed but increased." **— C.S. Lewis**

Love is a need that starts in the very core of our bodies and oozes out to every tiny cell that makes us, us. Countless movies, songs, and books have been written on the subject. It is a life-long quest for most of us—no, really all of us. Some yearn for it and some search far and wide for it. Still yet, some run from love. They run as fast and as far as they possibly can for many different reasons. Some people are afraid of it. Some feel and think they don't deserve it. Many have been hurt in the process of love, so they don't trust it. And there are even those who don't know how to love because they've never experienced it for themselves.

Love in its truest form is wise, but oh, the number of foolish decisions that have been made by scores of people in the name of love. Love also has enormous power but is often misunderstood. Love creates life. It is the very essence and reason for creation itself. But I'm going to go out on a limb and say that generally speaking, society doesn't have a clue as to what love really is. We are conditioned by pop culture, literature, and many other worldly influences to view love as an emotion. Everyone wants to experience as it is defined in the dictionary and many contemporary articles on love.

And to some extent, it is. But it is only a part of love. So in spite of the fact that society says our actions come from the feeling (emotion) of love, we need to understand that in actuality, God says that our actions should be the result of our love. It's choosing (making a conscious decision) to love.

We are given a choice—society's attitude toward love, or God's attitude toward love—but because God is love and because He created us with the ability and purpose to love, don't you think it only makes sense that his attitude is the one that serves us best? Of course, it is! And if you think about it, it's not all that difficult. This attitude of love God gives us in scripture says:

> "' Love the Lord your God with all your heart and with all your soul and with all your strength and with all your mind;' and, 'Love your neighbor as yourself'" **Luke 10:27**

Love God first and best and treat others the way you want to be treated. That's it. Nothing too hard about that, is there? If you live by this, you can't get it wrong. It even has provisions for you to watch out for yourself—to make sure you are being treated well. Do you see it?

When Jesus is telling us to love, he makes sure we know how important it is for us to be loved as well as give it. By telling us to love others as we love ourselves, Jesus is telling us we need to love ourselves. He wants us to know we deserve to be loved. But love does require you to be intentional. You have to think before you speak and act. You have to decide to love. Allow this attitude of love to consume your personal narrative.

First of all, you must decide to love God. One must love God with all that he or she has inside of them (with all their heart, soul, and mind). It starts by receiving God's love because he loved us first.

"We love because he first loved us." **1 John 4:19**

The second command is to love others as we (in the same way) love ourselves. Learning to love oneself happens best when we live with the realization that we are God's creation, and to not love ourselves is to disrespect God's creation. In turn, when we love ourselves, we become more compassionate, empathetic, and forgiving toward others because we know they are God's creation, too.

Without the right (God-defined) attitude and healthy understanding of love, anything we do or say in the name of love fails. It may not happen right away, but it will happen because worldly love doesn't last. Worldly love fails. Marriages collapse, friendships are severed, and parent-child relationships crumble.

Pride and arrogance erect a wall between that person and the Lord. Anxiety, depression, and low self-esteem carve a deep chasm between that person and the Lord. These things happen because worldly love isn't real love. Better said, it is not the most essential kind of love, agape love.

But what is real love? It's the age-old question we've been asking ourselves since the beginning of time. You can find the answer to this question in the Bible—and not just in one place. The Bible tells us about four different types of love; Eros - romantic love, Phileo - the love between friends, Storge - love between family members, and Agape – the unconditional love God has for us, and we should have for others.

Maybe you should explore the difference between the four. I believe that to have the best possible relationship with your significant other, all four types of love are coacting together. However, our interaction with ourselves and others we should develop understanding and focus on Agape love, unconditional love.

This is God's design and definition of love. This kind of love enables us to truly love God, ourselves, and others in the most real sense of the word. Authentic love. Therefore, to help you understand just what love really is, let's look at just a few examples of what the Bible has to say on the matter:

> "Love is patient and kind; love does not envy or boast; it is not arrogant or rude. It does not insist on its own way; it is not irritable or resentful; it does not rejoice at wrongdoing, but rejoices with the truth. Love bears all things, believes all things, hopes all things, endures all things. Love never fails" **1 Corinthians 13:4-7**

> "God is love. Whoever lives in love lives in God, and God in them" **1 John 4:16b**

> "But God shows his love for us in that while we were still sinners, Christ died for us." **Romans 5:8**

God is love. He didn't need us. But he wanted us. And that is the most amazing thing. – Rick Warren

I'll repeat it—from a world view, love is some grandiose emotion talked about and portrayed through our music, movies, and romantic novels. It is something that controls you. It's something that 'just happens.' Don't get me wrong I enjoy a good chic-flic. I've even been known to tear up on more than one occasion. My kids get a kick out of me, crying when I am watching movies. Hey, what can I say? I am a pretty sensitive guy.

But if Love was only an emotion that happens the way the world tells us, then how could it be fair for Jesus to command us to love one another? If love really 'just happens,' that wouldn't be possible? The fact is, love isn't just an emotion. We have complete control over whom we choose to love.

I can't say it enough: **the agape love that Jesus is referring to – is a decision.** And because love is a decision, the command we are given to love God, ourselves, and others is something we have to decide to do…or not.

God is love, and He offers this love freely and abundantly. It saddens me that humanity has a difficult time receiving it. We need to stop allowing our past, our weaknesses, and how others view us shape how we love God, ourselves, and others. We also need to learn to accept and embrace God's view of us and his love. When we have this attitude of love, we will begin to love God, ourselves, and others in such a way it will change us and the world around us. Through God's love, you are empowered to love yourself, and there is enormous power and peace in self-love.

The more we learn to love ourselves through Jesus Christ the more capable we are to love and serve others.

> "You can't touch it, but it affects how you feel. You can't see it, but it's there when you look at yourself in the mirror. You can't hear it, but it's there every time you talk about yourself. This important but mysterious thing is your self-esteem!" – **Author Unknown**

It has no power within itself, but it can cause you to shut down, or it can drive you. If you understand and grow your self-love, your self-esteem will grow as well.

Both Bret and JD tried to take their lives because they did not love themselves, nor could they forgive themselves. However, God's love is unconditional and will produce a healthy self-love if we embrace it. Do not be misled, though. Self-love is not *selfish* love.

I have had several of my Christian friends argue the point with me and tell me that we are to love others before ourselves and that loving ourselves before others is selfish. Then, of course, they quote Philippians 2:3, which says, *"consider others more important than yourself."* However, this very scripture, along with Jesus telling us to "love our neighbor as our self" in Luke 10:27, proves my point. If you do not love yourself or consider yourself to be necessary, then this sets the degree in which you can put others first and love others.

> "Self-love, as I understand the concept biblically and psychologically, includes the following: (1) accepting myself as a child of God who is lovable, valuable, and capable; (2) being willing to give up considering myself the center of the world; (3) recognizing my need of God's forgiveness and redemption." – **David Carlson**

The more you love yourself, the less reliant you are on others to love and affirm you. Loving yourself gives you a better sense of self-worth, removing or lessening the need to find your worth in someone or something else. As a result, you are better equipped to love others without having ulterior motives or expecting something in return.

Don't misunderstand what I'm saying. I'm not saying you should never expect to receive love and affirmation from others when you give the same to them. What you *shouldn't* do, however, is demand these things or make them a condition of your love. We are commanded by God to love—regardless of whether the person returns that love or not. We are commanded by God, even to love our enemies (Matthew 5:44).

I know this isn't easy, but when we understand love from God's perspective, we learn to love all people. We don't have to love their behavior or attitude, but we are commanded to love their person...their soul. We wish them no harm. We want them to know Jesus. We treat them kindly and with respect.

Loving someone in spite of their behavior is called grace—something we receive in continued abundance from God. We accept them just as they are and see them for who they can be—just like God does for us. For example:

If I have a friend who is a habitual liar, I will still love them as a person. I will have to verify everything they say rather than taking their word as truth. Or if my friend is a gossip, I will love them, but I will not confide in them. If a friend is a thief, I will not trust them around my valuables, but I will still love them.

The point I'm making here is that you can choose to love a person but do not have to approve of their destructive behavior nor allow their destructive behavior to drag you down. But yet, encourage and pray for them to overcome the destructive behavior.

The people the hardest to love are the ones who need it most.

Again, I know it's not always easy. Sometimes the people hardest to love are the ones who need it the most. There are also times we need to distance ourselves from certain people in certain situations so that we don't fall into their destructive pattern of behavior or allow their presence to be damaging to our wellbeing. By distancing ourselves, it can also help them see how wrong their behavior is. However, we can do this and still love them, pray for them, and have their best interests at heart.

When we have the right attitude about love, love becomes the core of our personal narrative. It is who we are—not what we feel. Loving God, yourself, and others will give you the confidence to overcome your issues and achieve your goals. Learn and choose to love. Go, and <u>be love</u> to others. It will bring great joy to your life. Love is the essence of life and the quintessence of God.

> "You will never look into the eyes of someone God doesn't love." **– Toby Mac**

LOVE

We must seek to love God, ourselves, and others, to the best of our ability. Love through your thoughts, your words, and your actions.

Attitude 3

Attitude of Grace and Mercy

Grace –

1. Favor or goodwill.
2. A manifestation of favor, especially by a superior.
3. Mercy; clemency; pardon.
4. Favor shown in granting a delay or temporary immunity.

Mercy –

1. Compassionate or kindly forbearance shown toward an offender, an enemy, or other person in one's power.
2. The disposition to be compassionate or forbearing.

Dictionary.com

> "The meaning of life. The wasted years of life. The poor choices of life. God answers the mess of life with one word: 'grace.'" – **Max Lucado**

Grace

A way to look at is, grace is receiving what we don't deserve, and mercy is not receiving what we do deserve.

When you find harmony in spite of chaos, you are experiencing grace.

Sometimes…often times in our lives, chaos and harmony collide. Searching for the harmony in spite of the chaos allows you to forgive yourself and know that any failure resulting from the chaos doesn't define who you are. When you find harmony in spite of the chaos, you are experiencing grace. You are *coacting* with grace.

Coacting with grace is a powerful weapon against the chaos of failure. By coacting with grace, you are using failure to empower you. That's right! Failure can empower! Here's how…

By coacting with grace instead of letting failure swallow us whole, we gain wisdom and endurance that moves us forward, allowing us to overcome and achieve. We use failure as a means of growth and learning instead of stagnation and defeat. Or, as one of my favorite quotes says: "We never fail. We either succeed, or we learn."

Allow failure to empower you!

When I fail—and trust me, I've done it more times than I care to count—I have to decide whether to be bitter, angry, cynical and play the blame game, or to take responsibility for my role in what happened and use it to grow and learn what to do, and what not to do the next time. In other words, I can let failure empower me or overpower me. The same is true with rejection, it can empower me or overpower me.

When I coact with God's grace, I become free from the chains of condemnation and the prison of shame and guilt. Grace allows me to dismiss condemnation and embrace conviction.

It truly is not about the do's and don'ts that we so easily get caught up in as we navigate through our faith or "religious journey." It is not about religion—it's about the relationship with God. Our do's and don'ts are the results of the relationship with God. Not the other way around.

Knowing this empowers me to transform condemnation, shame, and guilt into wisdom, knowledge, and insight. Grace strengthens me, preparing me to endure the trials and problems I face in life. But grace isn't just about me—what it gives me. No, receiving this life-changing grace should drive me to extend grace to others.

Therefore, when chaos and harmony collide, and failure seeps into your life. Embrace it…learn from it…grow from it…and allow it to build endurance. COACT WITH IT!

Mercy

While grace is receiving something good, but undeserved, (salvation and eternal life, being the most gracious gifts of all), mercy is the act of not having to suffer the consequences of our actions or getting the punishment we deserve (eternal death and separation from God, being the most obvious).

A prime example of mercy in my life is the fact that I have been pulled over for more traffic violations than I would like to admit—almost all of which were justified. I was guilty. But on many occasions, the officer let me go with nothing more than a warning. This was mercy. I deserved the ticket and did not get it.

The mercy I was shown can also be viewed as grace. The policemen graciously overlooked my lack of respect and negligence for the rules of the road. They gave me a gift I didn't deserve—the gift of not ticketing me.

The mercy and grace shown by the policemen in these situations have been deeply appreciated. It is nothing, however, compared to the mercy and grace, God extends to every single one of us.

The mere fact that we are allowed to be children of the living God signifies the depths of God's mercy and grace. He is merciful to forgive us of our sinful deeds. He is gracious in the fact that he welcomes us into his kingdom. The pairing of grace and mercy demonstrates why forgiveness is a significant attribute of having an attitude of grace and mercy. Neither grace nor mercy is even possible without forgiveness, which I'm sure is one reason we are commanded by God to forgive.

Forgiving Others

God's command to forgive is seen over and over again in the Bible. Forgiveness is at the core of grace and mercy.

> " And when you stand praying, if you hold anything against anyone, forgive them, so that your Father in heaven may forgive you your sins." **Mark 11:25**

Extending forgiveness to others is a must to receive forgiveness from God.

> "Be kind to one another, tenderhearted, forgiving one another, as God in Christ forgave you." **Ephesians 4:32**

> "Bearing with one another and, if one has a complaint against another, forgiving each other; as the Lord has forgiven you, so you also must forgive." **Colossians 3:13**

These two verses are the ultimate and original 'pay it forward.'

> "For if you forgive others their trespasses, your heavenly Father will also forgive you, but if you do not forgive others their trespasses, neither will your Father forgive your trespasses." **Matthew 6:14-15**

> "A new commandment I give to you, that you love one another: just as I have loved you, you also are to love one another." **John 13:34**

Again…if you want to receive forgiveness from God (and others) you have to give it, and this makes sense since we are to be like Jesus—the ultimate forgiver.

There are several reasons people have a hard time to forgive, but I want to mention two of them. First is I think people have a hard time forgiving because they are waiting to "feel" forgiveness for the person that has wronged them. Forgiveness isn't a feeling. It is a decision. We choose to forgive, regardless of how we feel. We can feel hurt—even anger—and still, forgive.

Secondly, people might think that trust and forgiveness are the same things. They are not. You can forgive someone and not trust them. When trust is broken, it has to be carefully mended and doesn't happen automatically or overnight. It takes time and a great deal of effort on the part of the one responsible for breaking someone's trust in them. You can forgive someone, yet not consider them someone you can confide in.

Feeling hurt and distrustful doesn't even mean you are going against 1st Corinthians 13—the 'part' that says love keeps no record of wrongs. Hurt and distrust are emotions. Forgiveness comes from an attitude of grace and mercy, and it is a decisive choice. The phrase itself essentially means love is not resentful—clearly indicating that forgiveness is involved. Just because someone has wronged you, does not mean you can't choose to love them and forgive them.

If someone wrongs me and I suffer from their actions, I can (and should) still choose to love and forgive them. I don't resent them. I simply set different boundaries for our relationship, and don't harbor any ill-will. I just don't confide in them as I once did until the trust is restored. My forgiveness is an extension of grace and mercy toward them because I know it is what God calls me to do, and because it is what he does for me.

Another characteristic of love that comes with an attitude of grace and mercy is "Love does not delight in evil." (1 Corinthians 13:6). Often times when we are hurt deeply by someone such as a cheating spouse, an unfair boss, or a deceptive family member or friend, we would be lying if we said we never had thoughts of wanting them to be held to the task, exposed for the hurtful person they are, or suffer some other consequence for their actions. Why not, right? They deserve it, don't they? Of course, they do! But that's not the attitude the Bible tells us to have.

> "Do not judge, and you will not be judged. Do not condemn, and you will not be condemned. Forgive, and you will be forgiven." **Luke 6:37**

Forgive them that harm you, set new boundaries, and move on. Let God take care of it.

> "Do not take revenge, my dear friends, but leave room for God's wrath, for it is written: "It is mine to avenge; I will repay," says the Lord." **Romans 12:19**

Forgiving Ourselves

We also must learn to forgive ourselves, which can often be more challenging to do than even forgiving others. Apply the previous words toward forgiving others to forgiving yourself. It's time to let go of some things. And give them to God. If He can forgive you—then you can forgive you.

> "I think that if God forgives us, we must forgive ourselves. Otherwise, it is almost like setting up ourselves as a higher tribunal than Him." **— C.S. Lewis**

I know this isn't easy to do. And truthfully, often we can't do it—not on our own, anyway. But with the help of the power of the Spirit living in us, we can. By coacting with God, we can. We can if we take every thought captive.

> "We take captive every thought to make it obedient to Christ." **2 Corinthians 10:5b**

Having an attitude of grace and mercy is an essential part of your personal narrative and will help you forgive yourself and others. It will bring great peace and joy to your life. It will also allow you to become more objective when overcoming your issues and achieving your goals.

> "God's mercy and grace gives me hope - for myself and for the world." **– Billy Graham**

GRACE

We must receive and walk in God's grace. Show grace to others through forgiveness. An unforgiving heart will rob you of the joy that life has to offer.

Attitude 4

Attitude of Gratitude

Gratitude –

1. The quality or feeling of being grateful or thankful.

Dictionary.com

"At times our own light goes out and is rekindled by a spark from another person. Each of us has cause to think with deep gratitude of those who have lighted the flame within us."
– Albert Schweitzer

What is gratitude? Most people would define gratitude as a feeling of thankfulness. After all, that's what you find in the dictionary. I would adventure to say that it is only partially correct, however, because genuine gratitude is the **attitude of thanks *to the point of showing* appreciation and returning the kindness that has been extended to you.**

> "So in everything, do to others what you would have them do to you" **Matthew 7:12a**

Gratitude in action is the Golden Rule. It is 'one good turn deserves another.' It is good stewardship. And in many ways, gratitude has an impact on whether or not God blesses us and how he goes about doing so. Yes, you read correctly—God's blessings have perimeters and even conditions. Some might say this statement contradicts the previous comments made by having an attitude of grace and mercy or also love.

God's love for us is unconditional; his grace and mercy are undeserving. His favor and blessing are different in that we must coact with God and strive for obedience. When we are disobedient, God often will remove Himself from our situation, not our life, but our situation until we surrender and repent.

Nevertheless, God is sovereign, and he will bless who chooses to. For the benefit of us as individuals and the betterment of the community and the world at large. God knows what he is doing. So trust him.

> "He causes his sun to rise on the evil and the good, and sends rain on the righteous and the unrighteous." **Matthew 5:45**

However, I do believe that when we are truly grateful for all that he gives us and does for us, it makes it quite a bit easier to be obedient. An attitude of gratitude creates a desire in us to respect God's word, honor Him, and follow Him.

Our faithfulness to Him in obedience to his commands, our stewardship, our willingness to live unashamedly for him, and our humility in recognizing that all we have belongs to God brings blessings upon our lives. When we live with the attitude of gratitude for our talents, material wealth, possessions, relationships, and health, God rewards us for this attitude by entrusting us with even more. The more gratitude we have towards God, the more God gives us to be grateful for.

> "Whatever you do, whether in word or deed, do it all in the name of the Lord Jesus, giving thanks to God the Father through him." **Colossians 3:17**

Gratitude teaches you to see everything for what it truly is… a gift from God.

No matter what you overcome or achieve in this life, if you do not have an attitude of gratitude, it won't matter. This includes everything—tangible and intangible. But here's the thing, having this attitude changes your perspective on life as well as the process you go through to overcome and achieve.

When you live with an attitude of gratitude, you learn to see everything for what it truly is—a gift from God. In turn, you are then able to give God the glory and honor He deserves for giving you these things. And when that happens, God gives you more to be thankful for…and the cycle continues. We should value and be more responsible for what God has blessed us with.

> "His master replied, 'Well done, good and faithful servant! You have been faithful with a few things; I will put you in charge of many things. Come and share your master's happiness!" **Matthew 25:21**

Gratitude for Trials

We even need to have an attitude of gratitude when life is rough, and the problems we face are painful and disruptive to our lives. When I say this, I'm not talking about being grateful that your spouse, child, or another loved one is suffering from a disease or passes away. I'm also not saying you have to be grateful for the heartache brought about by a rebellious child or the stress of unemployment or an unfaithful spouse.

What I'm saying is that we need to be grateful for what can come from these things—what *will* happen if you allow God to work in and through you. James, the brother of Jesus, explains it best when he says.

> "Consider it pure joy, my brothers and sisters, whenever you face trials of many kinds, because you know that the testing of your faith produces perseverance. Let perseverance finish its work so that you may be mature and complete, not lacking anything." **James 1:2-4**

Coact with Gratitude

> **The bad will ILLUMINATE the good.**

This perseverance James talks about is the road to overcoming and achieving. It is coacting with gratitude. It's implanting gratitude into our personal narrative. When we do this—when we coact with gratitude, when it is part of our personal narrative, we are better able to appreciate the blessings and good times because we know what it is like for those things to be absent from our lives.

JD lacked an attitude of gratitude that night, he almost took his own life. I believe, however, that falling so low and realizing God spared his life—it gave him a new appreciation for God and his own life. I know my experience in his ordeal significantly increased my faith and gratitude—especially when I found the silver dime lying on the ground.

But the feeling of gratitude isn't enough. If it is genuine gratitude, we need to express it somehow. One way I show my gratitude is by helping other people. Therefore, I am writing this book and Coactive Living as well as starting the Coactive Living ministry. These are just a few ways to express my gratitude for the many blessings that God has given me.

This isn't to say I don't ever struggle. We all do. But regardless of what we are facing, we should be thankful for every new day. So instead of dwelling on the negative, dwell on the positive and think about the things, situations, and people you have to be grateful for. The Bible teaches us to give thanks in all circumstances. All means all. So, when things don't go as planned—give thanks. When something bad happens—give thanks. When someone wrongs you—give thanks.

You may be thinking—really? I know it's not easy and may be hard to understand. But, give thanks to God that your circumstances are not worse than they are. Give thanks to God that things did not go as you had planned because God knows better. Again, in all things, give thanks. There have been many times in my life when God said NO! Trust me, I am thankful He did. I have also experienced many blessings from disparity and tragic events. Especially when I coact with these things.

Looking back, I am so grateful God says no.

I have had the amazing opportunity to take a road trip from California to Missouri and back on a few occasions with all of my kids together. I have also made that trip with each one of them individually. Looking back, I am so thankful to have experienced the opportunity. However, at the time of the road trips as a group and as individuals, each one came with their own unique set of problems.

Imagine being crowded in a vehicle for three days with three teenagers and two preteens. I loved it! But on the other hand, it had its challenging moments. Even to the point that I pulled my SUV over to the side of the road, I got out and just walked out into an empty field. I didn't say a word to my kids. I just did it. I'm sure they thought Dad had lost his mind. I'm even more convinced they knew I'd lost it when I just stood there in the middle of the field yelling and waving my arms around like a crazy person.

When I felt like the tension and frustration was gone, I stopped, turned around, walked calmly back to the vehicle, got in…and drove away. To this day, I have no idea what, if anything, the kids said to me about it. They were probably too shocked to say anything at all.

So why did I do it? To adjust my attitude, that's why. Even though I enjoyed each trip, and they were all special for different reasons, they weren't without their share of frustrations. If I hadn't gotten rid of my frustration the way I did, I would have taken it out on the kids, and the trip wouldn't have been near as fun and unique as it was.

If I didn't learn to adjust my attitude and be grateful throughout the years, I'm pretty confident I wouldn't have had the relationship with them that I did when they were growing up. And most likely, I wouldn't have the relationships I have with them now as adults. I am not implying that I have never lost it with my kids and acted a fool. I wish I could say I always remained calm, relaxed, and collect in dealing with my kids. Unfortunately, that's not the case, far from it.

I am extremely grateful for all of my children. They know I love them and will always be here for them. I would say that there is a high level of authenticity in my relationship with all four of my kids. As well as a sincere love.

When I visit them, in many ways, they make me feel welcome. Then like every family, on the other hand, we have our challenging moments. It's a uniquely beautiful thing. We enjoy hanging out together, and it is in large part because they know I am grateful for their presence in my life. I am thankful for their unique personalities and the unique perspective each one brings to my life. There is a fair share of things I just have to shake off. I am sure they feel the same way about me, especially when it comes to the "Dad talks" or "my dorkiness."

God has a uniquely beautiful relationship with each one of us.

God is the same way, you know. He accepts us and loves us for our unique personality. He has a uniquely beautiful relationship with each one of us. God also sees us for who we can be and is amazingly patient in waiting for us to allow Him to show us how to become that person. I am so grateful for that, aren't you? I am also thankful for the fact that His love, mercy, and grace are part of His gratitude toward us. Especially when we strive to become that person.

If you were to google the psychological benefits of gratitude, you would find many articles by doctors, therapists, and psychologists advocating the importance and benefits of gratitude. Personally, having an attitude of gratitude has been life-changing for me. I encourage you to embrace an attitude of gratitude. Pause for a minute and think of things in your life to be grateful for. Take another moment to thank God for all these things and ask him to teach you to be grateful for all things—the good and the bad. An attitude of gratitude should be paramount in your personal narrative.

> "The more you express gratitude for what you have, the more likely you will have even more to express gratitude for." **— Zig Ziglar**

GRATITUDE

We must live a life of gratitude. Be thankful for all that you have, and God will continue to bless you.

Attitude 5

Attitude of Humility

Humility –

1. Freedom from pride or arrogance: the quality or state of being humble.

Humble –

1. not proud or haughty: not arrogant or assertive
2. reflecting, expressing, or offered in a spirit of deference or submission a humble apology
3. to destroy the power, independence, or prestige of

Merriam Webster

> "I believe that the first test of a great man is his humility. I don't mean by humility, doubt of his power. But really great men have a curious feeling that the greatness is not of them, but through them. And they see something divine in every other man and are endlessly, foolishly, incredibly merciful." — **John Ruskin**

You never fail! You either succeed or you learn.

An attitude of humility leads to a teachable heart. When you have a teachable heart, your personal narrative can adapt to your circumstances and God's will. Also, you will live life with the perspective that you never lose; you either win or you learn.

You can learn from a two-year-old or overhearing a conversation in a coffee shop. The universe becomes a university. You will learn from music, movies, reading, and you can even learn from sitting watching a tree sway in the wind. You also learn from God and others.

Humility makes you more open-minded and better equipped to find solutions to overcome and achieve. Your overall attitude toward love and life is different than that of someone lacking in humility. An attitude of humility also leads to wisdom.

> "When pride comes, then comes disgrace, but with humility comes wisdom." **Proverbs 11:2**

So often, people try to **create** God's will in their lives based on what they believe to be best—instead of asking God to reveal his good and perfect will for their lives and guide them toward it. This is pride—not humility. If we humble ourselves before God, He will not only guide us in changing our personal narrative, but He will reveal to us His will for our lives.

Humility also makes it possible for us to submit to God and others. In humility, we seek to understand the thoughts and feelings of others, so we can love and serve them to the best of our ability. Humility allows us to learn and grow from our mistakes. It leads one to first seek to understand others.

> "If I were to summarize in one sentence the single most important principle I have learned in the field of interpersonal relations, it would be this: Seek first to understand, then to be understood." **Dr. Stephen R. Covey**

This quote is from 7 Habits of Highly Effective People by Dr. Stephen Covey. This was habit number five. Seek first to understand, then to be understood. When I read this, it changed my life.

Without an attitude of humility I don't how people can have an authentic love and live and authentic life.

Maybe this changing my life phrase is overused. But you have to realize that many things in life will alter your path and final destination, even our ultimate destination. Make no mistake our attitudes matter. Without an attitude of humility, I don't know how people can have an authentic love and live an authentic life.

It is humbling to know who I am in Christ and who I would be without Him. I am humbled and grateful for God's grace through Christ. I am nothing without Him. I don't say this lightly or with piety. My faith is secure, and my desire to be fully God's is strong. But I am weak in certain areas of my life, and many times my pride has been higher than my humility. So it is only by the grace of God that I can remain His. I regularly ask God to keep me humble and reveal it to me when pride seeps in.

I Love God, and I have a calling and a yearning in my heart to serve God and reach out to others. I yearn for this because of what God has done for me…because he has blessed me. I did not attend seminary, and I was one semester shy of finishing my B.A. degree in ministry at a Christian University.

To try to complete my degree would only serve to reaffirm my lack of ability to focus on my studies. Time and again, I allowed circumstances to launch me down the path of the Prodigal Son, so to speak, referring to my weakness with food. Also, as a single man, I had to deal with my perspective on dating and learn to respect and honor women as beautiful daughters of our lord. I never drink alcohol or do drugs, well I experimented with pot at age twelve for about six-months. I am just saying that alcohol and drugs are addictions I never have struggled with.

So as I wrote Coactive Living, I often asked who am I to write a book about God and Christian living? I have sin issues, I am a horrible speller, and my vocabulary and grammar are hideous in comparison to the many authors whose works fill our bookstores. Why would I even try?

I struggled with these questions and doubts for a very long time. Finally, however, it was revealed to me that these doubts are coming from faulty thinking, a false personal narrative. These thoughts are not from the Spirit that lives in me. I had to learn that my credentials don't come from books or even from myself. They come from God. I don't live to please man, but I live to please God.

So if my heavenly father is telling me to write Coactive Living and now this book, then I need to humble myself and write. What happens after I do is up to God. Just like everything else in my life is. Meaning, I do my part and let God do His. That's Coacting with God.

I will say that finally, after humbling myself and applying the principles of coactive living to my perspective on dating and women that I have had great success. Those that know me know this was a big accomplishment in my life.

Now it's time for me to be humble before God again and take responsibility for my physical health. Don't misunderstand. In comparison to our culture, I am average regarding my weight. However, the average male my age is overweight and unhealthy. I want to lose weight and get healthy so that I can be an example for the launch of my book Coactive Living and workbook series. I want to apply the coactive principles to my physical health like I have my mental and spiritual health. I want to be the best me possible, so I can focus more on others.

The point I'm making here is that we need to humbly seek God's will for our lives without worrying about what the world's perspective of what His plan might be or what people might think. God can work in and through us regardless of whether or not we have a formal education, skills, aptitude, or resources. Don't get me wrong—I am in no way discrediting those who have worked hard to achieve their educational and professional goals by doing what it takes to gain and advance their skill sets.

Having a formal theological degree or a preaching degree is invaluable in many situations. Maybe I'll finish mine someday. But education or no education, God can and will use you or me in a significant way if we humble ourselves before him and allow him to do so. It's about having the right attitude and desire to do God's will.

> "Humble yourselves in the presence of the Lord, and He will exalt you." **James 4:10**

> "Live in harmony with one another. Do not be proud, but be willing to associate with people of low position. Do not be conceited." **Romans 12:16**

"You are as good as the best – but no better than the rest."

Yes, if you humble yourself before God, He will lift you up. But know that your position in life, your gifts, and your resources can be gone at any time. There are no guarantees in life. Therefore, we should humbly do the best we can with what we have. Honor God and use these things for his purpose (which is to love and edify others).

If your understanding of what God's will is for your life does not incorporate the opportunity to love, encourage, and build others up through it, whether directly or indirectly, then I would question if it's truly God's will and encourage you to keep seeking.

Be careful, though, to never think that you are better than anyone else in God's eyes. "You are as good as the best—but no better than the rest," Jesus says what you did or did not do for the least of these you did or did not do to him.

> "Truly I tell you, whatever you did for one of the least of these brothers and sisters of mine, you did for me." **Matthew 25:40**

But, you ask, if no one is better than another, who is the 'least' of these? The 'least' are those who need help with material things. Uplift those who need to be emotionally and spiritually encouraged. Face it—there are those of us who have more than others. If you are one of the fortunate and see someone less fortunate, maybe a homeless person, a sick person, a socially awkward person, or even a mean, unkind person. Jesus is saying to treat them good. Having an attitude of humility will lead you down a path of treating all people with respect, love, and kindness. Everyone can use some encouraging words.

Who are we to say what they can and can't do for the Lord? Who are we to say who God will use or not use to carry out his ministry? You can have the highest position, all the wealth, and be extraordinarily gifted, and still, it will not matter compared to those who have nothing but yet humble themselves before our Lord and walk according to His will. If you do not humble yourself and love all people, you have nothing.

> "If I have the gift of prophecy and can fathom all mysteries and all knowledge, and if I have a faith that can move mountains, but do not have love, I am nothing." **1 Corinthians 13:2**

Pride

Pride, which is the opposite of humility, can indeed rob you of experiencing the joy that comes through following the lead of the Holy Spirit. There are many things the Spirit wants to show us and bless us with, but can't because our pride or ego is in the way. Often in dysfunctional relationships, pride is a significant factor preventing healthy resolutions. We must humble ourselves so that we will have a teachable heart, ears to hear, and eyes to see.

I learned a valuable lesson regarding pride during a men's retreat weekend—that weekend, God challenged my readiness to be in fulltime ministry. During the worship time at one of the evening services at this retreat, I was singing praises to God for all I was worth when God's voice clearly came to me. He softly and lovingly said to me, "Steve, fall on your knees and worship Me." Like I just said, when I heard this voice in my head, I knew without a doubt that it was God. But I became very nervous and began to look around the room. All the other men were standing and singing. No one else was on their knees. I thought to myself this would be embarrassing because I would be the only one doing it.

The voice said again, "Fall on your knees and worship Me." And again, I knew it was God speaking to me, but I still could not muster up the courage to do it. I couldn't stop thinking what the other men would think. I felt my face burning. I thought maybe if I lift my arms to the heavens and sing with more fervor and emotion that this would serve the same purpose.

A third time His voice rang out, "Fall on your knees and worship Me." This time I didn't look around the room. This time I didn't think what the other men might think. This time I responded with an emphatic yet fearful "No! I can't."

Immediately after I said those three words (half to myself and half out loud), the man directly beside me fell on his knees and began to worship God. I looked down at him with immeasurable shame in my heart. I felt weak in my knees. My heart was tremendously heavy and grew even heavier when men all over the room were falling on their knees to worship God. In just a short time, every man in the room was on their knees—including me.

As we continued to sing, I pleaded with God to forgive me. I couldn't stop crying. I knew what I had done. I also understood that I needed to deal with my pride if ever I wanted God to use me in fulltime ministry. Why should He use me in full-time ministry if I can't humble myself enough to be obedient enough to fall on my knees to worship Him?

God wanted to use me that day. He was allowing me the opportunity to lead the way to ignite a powerful and spirit-filled experience in that room full of men, to fall on our knees and humble ourselves before God, our King. God wanted me to experience what it would be like to lead the way and allow him to use me that day. But I didn't obey the call, so God used someone else more willing, and I missed out on a huge blessing. Who knows, maybe several men that day missed out on God's blessing.

How sad and painful those memories are even today! If the King of Kings and Lord of Lords can humble Himself to serve others, to wash His disciple's feet, and then die for each and every one of us, then who are we to not be humbled by what He did and obey his command to love one another or to do what He asks of us?

> "Now that I, your Lord and Teacher, have washed your feet, you also should wash one another's feet." **John 13:14**

Even in JD's situation. You might think, how much lower can one go than to be willing to take their own life? I am by no means an authority in understanding suicide or understand people who want to end their life. I am going to guess at some level humiliation is involved. It's not the same as of humility, by any stretch of the imagination. Humiliation is associated with self-loathing—self-hatred. Regardless, I am not trying to address the psychology or philosophy behind suicide.

Nevertheless, maybe JD was lacking an attitude of humility, which kept him from genuinely seeking help. Maybe pride was taunting him, saying, "How can you face life and others in your current situation?" The inability to be vulnerable and get the help we need with whatever the issue is it is generally an issue of pride—the lack of humility. Pride prevents vulnerability, and there are strength and power in being vulnerable.

> "Be completely humble and gentle; be patient, bearing with one another in love." **Ephesians 4:2**

> "Do nothing out of selfish ambition or vain conceit. Rather, in humility value others above yourselves." **Philippians 2:3**

> "God chose the lowly things of this world and the despised things—and the things that are not—to nullify the things that are, so that no one may boast before him." **1 Corinthians 1:28-29**

> "Humble yourselves, therefore, under God's mighty hand, that he may lift you up in due time. Cast all your anxiety on him because he cares for you." **1 Peter 5:6-7**

Having a personal narrative that embraces an attitude of humility is empowering. From it comes a serving and teachable heart that leads to wisdom.

> "When pride comes, then comes disgrace, but with humility comes wisdom." **Proverbs 11:2**

> Humility is not thinking less of yourself, it's thinking of yourself less. **– C. S. Lewis**

HUMILITY

We must seek humility. When we humble ourselves, it creates in us a teachable heart.

Attitude 6

Attitude of Acceptance

Acceptance –

1. the quality or state of being accepted or acceptable His theories have gained widespread *acceptance*.
2. the act of accepting something or someone: the fact of being accepted: APPROVAL *acceptance* of responsibility

Merriam Webster

"Acceptance of one's life has nothing to do with resignation; it does not mean running away from the struggle. On the contrary, it means accepting it as it comes, with all the handicaps of heredity, of suffering, of psychological complexes and injustices."
– Paul Tournier

For most of my life, I have suffered from psychogenic seizure disorder; and have been diagnosed with a slew of mental health issues, including PTSD and dissociative disorder. I go into more detail in my book Coactive Living.

I'll be going along with whatever activity I'm doing without anyone, including myself, noticing something is wrong. Then all of a sudden, it's like my brain reboots, and all my senses are in chaos. I lose the previous five or ten minutes of my life, I can't remember. My vision is like watching a 3D movie, or sometimes I get severe tunnel vision. Everything around me sounds muffled, or I can distinctly hear multiple conversations at the same time. I have the sensation of leaving my body.

Though I have chosen not to take medication for over 25 years now, this is still something I have to accept and deal with regularly. It has caused me to experience severe panic attacks, tonic-clonic seizures, hallucinations, and has been the source of significant anxiety in my life. For years I tried to figure out what was wrong and get rid of whatever 'it' was.

It was only then when I finally *accepted* the fact that this was a part of my life, then something changed inside of me. I *accepted* that I had to learn to live with my condition instead of trying to run from it. I learned to coact with it. I overcame the issue by mitigating the impact it had on my life as opposed to eradicating it. I still deal with my spells regularly, and I have one or two panic attacks a year, but nothing like it used to be.

> "Acceptance of what has happened is the first step to overcoming the consequences of any misfortune." **– William James**

When I realized how significant and impactful this revelation was in my life, I then started looking at other areas of my life that I needed to accept. For example, my father not telling me he loved me. I learned to accept that that is just who he is. By accepting him for who he is as well as accepting certain things without making judgments against him, I have been able to shift my focus away from the negative impact these things were having on my life and my relationship with my father.

This is also true of my four grown kids. I had to accept that their life choices are theirs. It's their journey, not mine. It's between them and their Heavenly Father. I accept the mistakes I made as a parent as well as accepting the successes I had as a parent. I love them no matter what, and I'm their biggest fan.

Acceptance can often be a difficult thing to do. Acceptance is to come to recognize or admit your circumstance and thoughts as valid. Also, other people and their circumstances are valid. As well as their thoughts and feelings.

Acceptance does not mean that you approve of the circumstances you are in or approve of another person's behavior. Acceptance will also help you determine what is true and what is not.

I shared this in the attitude of love, but it had such an impact on my life it bears repeating, if I have a friend who is a habitual liar, I will still love them as a person. I will just have to verify everything they say rather than taking their word as truth. Or if my friend is a gossip, I will love them, but I will not confide in them. If a friend is a thief, I will not trust them around my valuables, but I will still love them.

> "Accept one another, then, just as Christ accepted you, in order to bring praise to God." **Romans 15:7**

With an attitude of acceptance, my personal narrative tells me to accept the person but do not let their bad behavior drag me down. Again, accept the problem as the problem, not you or them as the problem.

I agree that these circumstances are in my life and other's lives. Now that I recognize and admit it, what should I do about it, or how should I respond? Again, you can recognize and acknowledge that a person is in your life, but you do not have to agree with them.

Approve of the person as one that is loved by God but not approve of their behavior. However, you should love them none the less. Now that you recognize this, you should pray and think about how to respond to them in a healthy way.

This is true of yourself as well. If there is something about yourself that you do not like, accept it for what it is. But, do not allow it to hinder the love you have for yourself. For example, I have overcome many things in life. But I find that one of the biggest struggles I have is eating healthy and proportionately. In other words, I am physically unhealthy and about twenty-five pounds overweight.

Now I accept this fact, but I don't like it. You see, I can accept the fact that I'm overweight and unhealthy, but I don't have to like it. And if I don't like it, then I can choose to do something about it. I can choose to lose weight and get healthy again. I can choose to apply the principles of Coactive Living to this area of my life. I can decide to make healthy lifestyle changes. I have experienced much success with these principles in so many other areas of my life, I know they work.

Although I have accepted being unhealthy even though I don't like it—it doesn't affect the love I have for myself. It does not have to rob me of my joy in life. Or affect some of the other areas of my life. Remember, you are not the problem. The problem is the problem. Because I fully accept myself as a child of God and receive all the benefits that come with it. Such as understanding that these seven attitudes are the charter traits of Jesus Christ. Because I do love myself, through Christ, I am empowered and equipped to deal with "the problem."

If I were not to accept my weight issue as the problem and continue to say that I am the problem, I would internalize it as opposed to being more objective about it. Then this would have more impact in other areas of my life. Such as my self-esteem. It can cause me to experience more depression. I would also probably have a faulty perception of how people view me, which could cause anxiety. This is just the starting point of the snow-ball. Again, being overweight should not and does not rob me of my joy regarding my identity and who I am as a person.

Accepting Joy

> **Accept the gift of joy and live it out daily**

The same is true for you. Don't let your circumstances rob you of your joy. Life, Satan, or any person does not have the authority to take your joy. God gave it to you through the Holy Spirit, and He is not taking it back. Whether you live it out or not is up to you, you have free will and get to choose to live a joyful life or not. It's a gift that God gave to you for accepting His son as your personal savior. It is a part of your identity. Therefore, accept the gift of joy and live it out daily.

Keep in mind joy and happiness are not the same. Joy comes from within your being, and happiness is dependent on how you respond to your happenstances. Happiness and happenstances both come from the same root word hap, which means chance or luck. Joy can lead to happiness. However, I would venture to say that happiness does not lead to joy. Yet, you have the power to choose to be joyful and happy regardless of your happenstances.

Please don't misunderstand me. Being unhealthy and overweight is not a good thing. I will reap what I sow. I will pay the consequences of being overweight, which is increasing my odds of having a shorter life, it hinders the things that I want to do in life, my activities. And, being single, well, it will have an impact in this area of my life as well.

My friend Mark and I were having a conversation about this topic. He said, "You can be overweight and sad, or you can be overweight and happy." I believe there is a lot of truth in this statement. Especially when it comes to joy.

Accept Your Identity

Regardless of my outward appearance, my weaknesses—I am a child of God! I am a child of God who struggles with food and is overweight. And as a child of God, I have accepted the Holy Spirit that lives in me. As a result, the fruit of this is love, joy, peace, patience, kindness, goodness, faithfulness, gentleness, and self-control. You see, being overweight doesn't deny me of these precious gifts of the Spirit. My circumstances do not rob me of these gifts that God has given me.

Therefore, I will accept the fact that I have a problem with my weight and deal with accordingly to the best of my ability through prayer and by coacting with God. I will also accept these fantastic gifts from the Spirit and live them out in my life. In spite of my weaknesses.

Now I know some of you are thinking, wait! What about self-control? Isn't that a fruit of the Spirit? YES. I am so grateful for this. I exercise self-control in many other areas of my life. My negative thinking, my anger, and speaking truth, not judging others, and loving all people—just to name a few. Again being single, self-control plays a big part in my life. Dating can be complicated. This was an area of my that was problematic for me. I had to accept this fact. With an attitude of acceptance also came surrendering and accepting the power of the Holy Spirit to help (self-control.)

I hope and pray to experience the same success in weight management and acquiring a physically healthy lifestyle. Again, regardless of my success in this area or any other areas of struggle or sin—God loves me just the same and accepts me just as I am.

> "But the fruit of the Spirit is love, joy, peace, forbearance, kindness, goodness, faithfulness, gentleness and self-control. Against such things there is no law." **Galatians 5:22-23**

When you accept life's circumstances and accept yourself and other people in your life just as they are without judgment, you increase your ability to navigate through your circumstances and enhance your relationships. Especially when you are coacting with the Holy Spirit.

Letting go of the struggle

Letting go of the struggle is also a part of having the attitude of acceptance. Quite honestly, again, not always so easy to do. When we find ourselves in a situation that makes us uncomfortable or threatened, we tend to 'freeze, fight, or flight.' But none of this is necessarily letting go.

> "Some people believe holding on and hanging in there are signs of great strength. However, there are times when it takes much more strength to know when to let go and then do it." – **Ann Landers**

For example, I was seeing my psychologist trying to work through my seizure and panic issues, the doctor stood up and handed me one end of a scarf, and she kept the other. I willingly coacted with her by doing what she asked and by having a humble and teachable heart as she led me through the following 'exercise.'

She told me to imagine the scarf was a rope. Next, she said to pretend that she was a monster and that between us were jagged cliffs and a drop off of hundreds of feet. The Psychologist told me that both the 'monster' and I were trying to pull each other off the side of the cliff. However, it soon becomes evident that the monster is stronger than me and will easily pull me over the cliff.

"What are you going to do?" she asked.

I responded without hesitation that I would let go of the rope. "That's right," she replied. "Let go of whatever struggles you have like they are ropes with a monster tugging on the other end."

She continued to say, "Now, you have all this freedom to move around on your side of the cliff even though the monster is still there."

I know that sounds overly simplistic, but it worked, or at least it does most of the time. You see, fighting feeds the monster. Just having that visual picture in my mind helps. **Accepting** that my "spells" my "seizures" were real and present, seeing them for what they were, and letting go of the struggle significantly lessened the power they had over me. I was able to see the problem as the problem and concentrate on solutions. Here is the progression. You stop focusing on the person or the issue, and you accept the problem as the problem, then you focus on the solution, and respond accordingly.

> "Christian faith does not involve repressing one's anxiety in order to appear strong. On the contrary, it means recognizing one's weakness, accepting the inward truth about oneself, confessing one's anxiety, and still to believe, that is to say that the Christian puts his trust not in his own strength, but in the grace of God. **– Paul Tournier**

In the specific case of my seizure disorder, the solution was to realize it isn't going away and to adapt to it by managing my surroundings in such a way that the possibility of having a seizure is significantly reduced. For me, this means keeping my exposure to fluorescent lighting to a minimum. So what if I can't go to Target or spend much time in Walmart or most other stores for very long without having a spell! It's not the end of the world. It's my life. But I can still live a meaningful and productive life. I know that now.

I no longer allow my condition to keep me from focusing on what matters and on who I am in God's eyes. No longer am I allowing my disorder to be the enemy's way of dividing my attention and distracting me away from where my focus should be. When I let go of the struggle and started holding on to God, my life changed. The spells became much less substantial, and achieving my goals became more significant.

ACT – Acceptance and Commitment Therapy is one of the four therapy models I used for research in my book Coactive Living.

> "Acceptance – Whether it be a situation you cannot control, a personality trait that is hard to change or an emotion that overwhelms, accepting it can allow you to move forward. Obsessing, worrying, and playing things over and over keep you stuck. In this sense, asking *why* can leave you helpless. ACT invites you to accept the reality and work with what you have.
>
> Some acceptance strategies include:
>
> 1. Letting feelings or thoughts happen without the impulse to act on them.
> 2. Observe your weaknesses, but take note of your strengths.
> 3. Give yourself permission to not be good at everything.
> 4. Acknowledge the difficulty in your life without escaping from it or avoiding it.
> 5. Realize that you can be in control of how you react, think, and feel."
>
> **– Deborah Serani Psy.D.**
> **– Psychology Today Article**

Having an attitude of acceptance has helped me mitigate many issues in my life. An attitude of acceptance is also applicable to positive things in life. Blessings. Sometimes we feel like we don't deserve good things. Accepting the good things in life is just as important as learning to accept your adversities and challenges.

The most important thing you will ever accept in life is God's love and His gracious gift of salvation. It's completely free and motivated by the love of God. Many people have a hard time believing this and accepting this.

> "For God so loved the world that he gave his one and only Son, that whoever believes in him shall not perish but have eternal life." **John 3:16**

The other part of accepting salvation is accepting the fact that by doing so, you become a child of God. Being a child of the living God, the King of Kings, the Lord of Lords, comes with many blessings. There are a lot of people that can accept salvation and believe in God. But, for whatever reason, they have a difficult time accepting their position as a child of God. They have a difficult time accepting His love and the many blessings that come with it.

Accepting all your situations, both good and bad, will allow you to be more objective and able to turn your circumstances into blessings for yourself and others. Your bad situations in life will teach you and become a point of empathy for others in the same situations that you have overcome. They will also make you a stronger person and make you wiser. When your situations in life are good, they will allow you to be grateful and bless and edify others.

By having a personal narrative that embraces the attitude of acceptance, will change your life for the better. It will bring peace, love, and joy into your life. Accept who you were created to be. Accept whatever life puts before you.

An attitude of acceptance will enable you to accept responsibility for your misconduct, accept others without judgment, and accept your circumstances in life. Most importantly, accept God's Love and His amazing gift of salvation along with His help and blessings.

JD did not fully accept and embrace these amazing gifts from God. He did not accept his situation in life in a healthy way, if he did, he would have dealt with it and faced it head-on. His answer was not to accept it and just end it.

However, I did accept the truth of God's word on his behalf. I prayed for him, I ministered to him the best I knew how. I loved him as God had commanded me to do, I hoped for him. As a result, God spared his life and blessed me with answered prayer and a silver dime to remind me.

It is what it is – now what?

Remember accepting other people without judgment and the challenging things in life that may seem difficult does not mean that you are ok with it.

It merely says, "It is what it is – now what?"

> "Accept – then act. Whatever the present moment contains, accept it as if you had chosen it. Always work with it, not against it."
> **– Eckhart Tolle**

ACCEPTANCE

We must accept God's love and grace. When we learn to accept ourselves and our circumstances as is, we can then move forward and grow. We must also accept others without judgment.

Attitude 7

Attitude of Perseverance

Perseverance –

1. Steady persistence in a course of action, a purpose, a state, etc., especially in spite of difficulties, obstacles, or discouragement.
2. Theology, continuance in a state of grace to the end, leading to eternal salvation.

Dictionary.com

"Nothing in the world can take the place of persistence. Talent will not; nothing is more common than unsuccessful men with talent. Genius will not; unrewarded genius is almost a proverb. Education will not; the world is full of educated derelicts. Persistence and determination alone are omnipotent. The slogan, 'press on' has solved, and always will solve, the problems of the human race."
– Calvin Coolidge

I assure you, my life has been riddled with challenges, and I have had to persevere through many things. Some things brought on by myself and other things out of my control. However, I always have control over how I respond to them.

Thinking about your challenges, and knowing the stories of others, one basic fact of life should become abundantly clear: life has its share of problems. Falling upon hard times to one degree or another is inevitable. Personally falling apart when these things happen, however, is not… inevitable, that is…

We don't have to let these things stop us in our tracks. We can, by the grace of God, persevere. God didn't create us with a spirit of timidity 2 Timothy 1:7. Giving up isn't what we've been designed to do. God created us with a brain that is creative and intelligent. He created us to persevere instead of throwing in the towel. Don't misunderstand. There are times when it's time to give up on certain goals and change direction. But, the vast majority of the time, when we do, it's premature. If we do quit, we should only do so by the instruction of the Lord.

The urge to give up on your goals and dreams, your calling, your marriage, your kids, and your career is a seed Satan plants in your mind either directly or indirectly through your flesh. Yes, Satan is real, my friend, and the spiritual battle that we must endure is real as well. In Coactive Living, I go into more detail on the spiritual battle—the battle of the mind.

Therefore, give this due diligence in your personal narrative. If you don't, you will start to live with a faulty personal narrative. Satan will try to deceive you into believing you can't get through the challenges of life—to overcome your issues and achieve your goals. He will tempt you with thoughts like –you don't deserve it. No one cares. You aren't smart enough, sexy enough, or worthy enough. He will use people and circumstances to try to drag you down and get you to quit. Has he succeeded in doing this to you? Have you given up?

If so, stop thinking this way and start persevering. Change your personal narrative, and keep on keeping on! Know that you have all authority over Satan and the flesh through the power of Jesus Christ.

Dialectics – Conflict

Another concept I go into in my book Coactive Living is dialectics. It's not a very common word. However, the concept is important, and I encourage you to learn the word and contemplate its meaning. This concept goes all the way back to Aristotle and Plato. It is also used in Dialectic Behavioral Therapy (DBT).

Dialectic means conflict or opposition. It is the opposing and conflicting interactions we have with God, ourselves, others, and life. Dialectical exchanges happen in our lives and all around us regularly. The world and life are dialectic—full of conflict and opposition, and it's actually necessary.

"For example, what would light mean without understanding darkness, what would wetness mean to a fish who had never experienced anything else, what would blue mean in an all blue world, what would inhibition mean without appreciating what complete disinhibition looks like? Dialectics breaks down our concepts into their seemingly opposite parts–viewed another way, as thesis, antithesis, and synthesis…

In fact, the only way to understand most concepts, and possibly existence itself, relies on the fact that the world is constructed and perceived around seemingly polar opposites. There's just one problem here–the term opposite often seems to imply completely different, antagonistic, and utterly irreconcilable. But from ancient Eastern mysticism to modern day physics, we now know that simply isn't the case. What look like totally opposite ideas usually contain at least some element of truth representing the other side of an argument or idea. Knowing that fact can be woven into therapy to help people understand where others are coming from and make attempts at finding an integrated, middle ground when conflict arises."

Charles Elliott, Ph.D. and Maureen Lassen, Ph.D.

Often we have a better understanding of a concept, idea, or our own emotions because of knowing its opposition. For example; how would you fully know and understand happiness without sadness, warm without cold, good without bad, and so forth. Conflict is the very thing that prepares us to experience life to its fullest.

Every problematic situation and every tragedy you have encountered can work to strengthen your spirit, body, and mind. These things can make you a better and stronger person. When you persevere, you overcome. And when you overcome, you achieve. Therefore, persevere.

> "Through whom we have gained access by faith into this grace in which we now stand. And we rejoice in the hope of the glory of God. Not only so, but we also rejoice in our sufferings, because we know that suffering produces perseverance; perseverance, character; and character, hope. And hope does not disappoint us, because God has poured out his love into our hearts by the Holy Spirit, whom he has given us." **Romans 5:2-5**

Don't Quit

When you have an attitude of perseverance, quitting isn't an option.

> Keep on keeping on.
> **Don't Quit!**

Referring to life, and overcoming your issues and achieving your goals. Don't give up on life and moving forward. Like I said earlier, some things you have to let go of, but that doesn't mean quit.

When you have an attitude of perseverance, you have hope—a hope that, according to scripture, will not disappoint (Romans 5:5). When you have an attitude of perseverance, it isn't about can or can't. It's about will or won't. I heard in a movie, "Can't' lives on 'won't' street."

Things may not always turn out the way you think they should, but when you persevere with God in the lead, you learn and grow from your hardship. So instead of running or burying your head in the sand, keep going. **Don't quit on life.** With God, there is nothing you can't overcome.

JD tried to quit on life and gave up. He didn't want to persevere any longer. His personal narrative guided him to an isolated parking garage where he attempted to end it all and made the final decision to give up on life. This was JD's solution. His truth, which wasn't the truth at all, was his life was not worth living any longer. However, the real truth, God's truth was that it was. Therefore, by the grace of God and the leading of the Holy Spirit, myself and the police officer persevered through the situation, and JD's life was spared.

Having an attitude of perseverance is also a way to share the truth of the Gospel with others. When people see the quality of perseverance in you, they will ask you what makes you this way. And when they do, you need to be ready to give them an answer. Your answer may very well be the beginning of their walk with the LORD.

> "Therefore, since we are surrounded by such a great cloud of witnesses, let us throw off everything that hinders and the sin that so easily entangles. And let us run with perseverance the race marked out for us" **Hebrews 12:1**

Perseverance can also be defined as embracing the process of overcoming your trials and tribulations and looking forward to the result. The term 'embracing the process' is a positive one, don't you agree? Embracing the process requires you to hurdle obstacles, face adversities, and overcome your fears. When you do these things, guess what? You are coacting with Jesus, persevering through life.

> "I can do all this through him who gives me strength." **Philippians 4:13**

Ironically, while I was writing this section on perseverance, I got a phone call from my youngest son. When I answered, he told me in a strained and broken voice that he was pretty sure he'd just broken some ribs. My two sons—both of whom have done MMA (Mixed Martial Arts) were currently in jujitsu—they were practicing for an upcoming tournament. While grappling with each other, my younger son landed wrong, possibly breaking his ribs.

After telling me what happened, I talked to him about persevering—not giving up and not letting this (possible) setback cause him to give up. I knew he had no intention of giving up, but I said it anyway. I couldn't help it—it's the dad in me. I just had to be sure he wasn't going to let the fear of pain or being defeated prevent him from doing his level-best to succeed. I encourage this in all of my children. My older son made some bad choices and had to spend a few years in prison. He persevered. My older daughter got involved in an unfortunate relationship, which ended with the guy breaking into her home and beating her up. She persevered. My younger daughter has had to persevere through some situations that came out of dysfunctional relationships as well. We all have had things that we had to persevere through.

> "I have seen something else under the sun:
> The race is not to the swift
> or the battle to the strong,
> nor does food come to the wise
> or wealth to the brilliant
> or favor to the learned;
> but time and chance happen to them all.
>
> Moreover, no one knows when their hour will come:
> As fish are caught in a cruel net,
> or birds are taken in a snare,
> so people are trapped by evil times
> that fall unexpectedly upon them."
> **Ecclesiastes 9:11-12**

Commitment and Courage

Whatever happens in life or any endeavor that we take on, stuff happens—keep on keeping on!

Perseverance requires commitment and courage. Commitment is the quality of being dedicated, while courage is the ability to do something even in the midst of fear. Fear from one degree to another is usually attached to setbacks, pain, failure, even success. Fear, if not dealt with appropriately, will hinder your attitude of perseverance.

I encourage you to embrace your fear…coact with your fear. Coacting with your fear gives you the courage to move forward in spite of your fear. You acknowledge it, but you don't entertain it. When you fail to coact with your fear, it always becomes bigger and scarier than it really is. Unless you coact with your fear, you won't be able to know its source and how to deal with it. Coacting, or persevering in spite of your fear doesn't always mean fear ceases to exist. It simply says you have chosen not to let your fears get the best of you.

> "I learned that **courage** was **not the absence of fear**, but the triumph over it. The brave man is **not** he who does **not** feel afraid, but he who conquers that **fear**."
> **– Nelson Mandela**

When you are committed to something, you are dedicated to overcoming whatever issues you encounter and are dedicated to achieving the goal regardless of your setbacks. You are committed to persevering. In the same way, you have the courage to persevere through your fears.

> "Most people fail not because of a lack of desire but because of a lack of commitment."
> **– Vince Lombardi**

An example of what it means to persevere is my book Coactive Living. I have been working on the concept of coactive living and writing the book for about fifteen years now. My thoughts are that it should have been completed a long time ago. For more reasons than I can count, though, it wasn't. But I have persevered through every single situation instead of letting the enemy (Satan) rob me of the blessing and joy of doing what I know God wants to do through me with this book. I assure you, I've had more than a few episodes of doubt. What if no one reads it? What if no one 'gets it'? What if someone reads it but thinks it has nothing of value to offer?

Believe me, when I say this, there are people out there that will feed these negative thoughts even more if you let them. In my case, it's Joel, the window cleaner. He is a very pessimistic person and tells me straight out that there is no way I will ever succeed with this book. Maybe he is right. I don't know. But I do know that I am coacting with God, and it's in God's hands. As for Joel, well, he does not believe there is a God. Or, according to him, he isn't smart enough to make that kind of decision. Therefore, he chooses not to have a relationship with God.

On another day, I was thinking differently. What if people do read it AND find it helpful? What if my efforts accomplished through humble perseverance help bring someone to Christ? Or better equip them to have a blessed joy-filled life. These thoughts brought me to my knees in humility and also caused a few knots in my stomach when I thought about the responsibility that goes with something like this.

I started to panic…a little. Then I realized that I was thinking exactly the way I am trying to teach you not to do. I wasn't supposed to panic. I reminded myself that I was supposed to coact with Jesus. So that's what I'm doing. I accepted my fear, and I am using it to empower me to do what God has called me to do. I am confident that no matter what happens, I am coacting with my Lord and Savior to overcome and achieve God's will for my life. And in doing so, I pray I can help you do the same.

Whatever it is that you are going through in life, always remember "without the test, there is no testimony."

> "Because you know that the testing of your faith produces perseverance. Let perseverance finish its work so that you may be mature and complete, not lacking anything." **James 1:3-4**

You must want it bad enough to persevere. Be courageous and keep on going! You will not regret it.

> "Many of life's failures are people who did not realize how close they were to success when they gave up." **–Thomas Edison**

Perseverance

We must not quit! Keep on keeping on.

Epilogue

I hope you can see why I chose these seven attitudes to represent a coactive life. There are many other quality and valuable attitudes to benefit you in life. However, I think these attitudes that you just read about will significantly change your life. They have mine. They have become a part of my core beliefs—a natural part of my personal narrative. I hope that you will strongly consider embracing and learning, no mastering these attitudes. I hope you will experience how these attitudes will benefit you in the process of overcoming your issues and achieving your goals.

Many of these attitudes may be defined as an emotion or have a significant emotional component to them. However, it is important, no—it is essential to understand that these life-changing attitudes are decisions. We have the ability to choose and live by each and every one of them. We can choose to search for the truth, speak the truth, and live the truth. We can choose to love God, ourselves, and others. We can choose to receive, give, and walk in grace and mercy. We choose to forgive ourselves and others. We choose to be grateful and live humbly before our God. We choose to accept God and his salvation. We choose to accept others without judgment, and whatever life brings our way. Then we choose to persevere through all of life's challenges.

> "He has told you, O mortal, what is good; and what does the Lord require of you but to do justice, and to love kindness, and to walk humbly with your God? **Micah 6:8**

In spite of what the world says, we are to live our lives based primarily on thoughts. Healthy thinking—not feelings. Healthy thinking is necessary for healthy emotions.

The flesh acts according to our feelings that are often provoked by faulty thinking. This is also the way of the world. That's one reason the divorce rate is so high. Have you ever heard; "I just don't love them anymore." This statement is coming from a personal narrative that allows their emotions to guide and dictate their actions as opposed to having a personal narrative that is governed by the Spirit of God and being intentional in making good decisions.

Choices lead to experiences—the emotional rewards are the result of our initial choices.

Again, we have free will to choose our attitude. When we live this way—according to God's instruction (vs. our feelings), we will experience his fruit…his blessings.

> "Because free will, though it makes evil possible, is also the only thing that makes possible any love or goodness or joy worth having." **— C.S. Lewis**

Well, you have read JD's story, and I hope you can see how these attitudes could have changed his life. Now I would like to share a personal story of mine regarding some of my journey as it relates to these attitudes.

After experiencing my divorce with my wife and remembering what it was like when my mom and dad divorced, I knew I had to be there for my kids. It was just something I had to do—for them and…for me. I reaped the consequences of my parent's divorce—just like my kids reaped the consequences of my actions and my divorce.

I was very involved and saw my kids regularly while they were children. Unfortunately, there were a few gaps in time during my two younger children's teen years that circumstances kept me from living nearby. However, our contact was very consistent. Looking back I wished I had been more diligent in figuring out a way to have lived closer to them.

After my parent's divorce, my father and I did not see much of each other or talk much. As I got older, I realized that it was more my fault than my father's. He tried to stay in contact with me, but I was not willing to do so. What can I say? I was twelve, and selfishly did not want to live by his rules. I wish now that maybe he would have forced the issue a little more, but I would have probably just pushed back that much harder, so I cannot truthfully and justifiably blame my dad for our lack of a relationship.

It did, however, cause me to work hard to be the most engaged father I could possibly be, so if nothing else, I learned the value of being engaged with my kids from my experience with my dad.

I am also happy to say that since my childhood, things had changed between my dad and me. A few years after my divorce and my mother's death, I began to take my children back to Missouri, where I grew up and where my father and family lived so that we could attend our annual family reunion. The kids loved it as much as I did, and over the years, we've made a lot of great memories both in our travels and at the reunion. My family has always shown my kids and me a lot of love—including my dad, the best he knew how.

As I observed my father around my kids and his other grandkids at family functions, I soon realized that he was not the same father I remembered him to be. Yes, he was still an old-school rancher/farmer kind of man; tough as the bulls he owned and didn't show his emotions, but he was good to them.

I still can't remember my dad saying he loved me or remember him ever hugging me, ever. But I stopped holding that against him. I stopped doing that the day I asked him what his parents (my grandparents) were like—what it had been like for him growing up. He looked at me and said, "Son, it was like I was just a hired hand on the farm." After that, I realized he didn't know how to say or do those things or even why they were so important because he probably never heard those words or gotten a hug himself.

But once I had kids of my own, I promised myself I would do things differently…a lot differently. I hugged my kids often as they were growing up and always told them that I loved them no matter what. I still do those things regardless that they're grown, and there is some distance between us.

Even though I no longer resented my dad's lack of emotional connectivity, a big part of me still wanted to hear those words come out of his mouth—the words "I love you." But what was even more important to me was for my dad to know I loved him. Yes, I hoped when I told him he would say it back, but regardless of whether he did or not, I wanted…no, I needed him to know what I thought and how I felt. So I made up my mind that when I saw him at the next family reunion, I was going to say, "Dad, I love you."

Being able to say this was a huge deal to me, so I asked the guys in the Bible study group I was leading, to pray about the situation. But me being me, I didn't do it. I had the opportunity to tell my dad I loved him, but like so many other times when I knew God was calling me to say or do something, I didn't have the courage or faith to obey. And in this instance, the timing and 'mood' were perfect, but I chickened out.

The next year rolled around and I…chickened out again. The third-year…and even a fourth year rolled around, and I still chickened out!

The fifth-year came, and I again asked my Bible study group to pray for me to have the courage to follow through. By this time, my kids were older—old enough to understand why I needed and wanted to say these words to my dad. I asked them to pray for me, too. I asked them to pray that God would give me the courage to tell their Papa that I loved him.

We arrived in Missouri ready for some good, quality family time. I was also confident that I would get time alone with Dad to tell him. However, two weeks went by without us ever having any time alone. So, I said nothing. But on the last day, we were there, I asked my brother if he would take the kids and me to where Dad was working that day so we could say goodbye. I told my kids that this was it—this was the day I was going to tell my dad I loved him.

Though my Dad was raising cattle and hay, he would take a contractor job here and there running a construction site. On that particular day, this is what he was doing; managing a remodel of a portion of a local shopping mall. When we got there, he was standing outside with four other construction workers standing around him.

There was no way I was going to tell him in front of everyone. I couldn't do it. We had all exchanged some small talk, said our goodbyes, and were walking to the car to leave for the airport. We were almost to the car when my youngest daughter, nine-years-old at the time, tugged my arm to get my attention and said, "Dad, you didn't tell papa that you loved him." The tears in my eyes started to build up as my heart, which was already heavy with regret, fell to my stomach. I knew if, for no other reason than my kids' sake, I had to go back and tell him. So I did.

I went back, and there he stood all alone. I went to him and said. "Dad, this is very hard for me to say, and I have tried for a long time now. But I want you to know that I love you."

I was both relieved and scared of what his response was going to be. He looked at me and gave me a friendly backhanded tap on my upper arm and said. "I appreciate that, son. Well, you have a safe trip back." Then he turned and walked away.

I questioned myself, that's it? Just "I appreciate that"? I'd told myself I didn't care whether he said it back or not, but at that moment, I did care. I cared a lot. But there was nothing else to say or do, so I started walking away, too. I hadn't gone very far when I heard my dad call out, "Son." I stopped, turned around, and looked. He was looking at me and said, "I love you too."

I wanted to cry right then and there. But I didn't want to cry in front of him, so I said, "Thanks, we'll see you." But the interesting thing is that I felt more relieved than happy. I was so relieved that I'd finally done what I'd been trying and planning to do for years. And what's more—it had gone exactly how it needed to! But the feeling of happiness from hearing my dad say that he loved me didn't come until later.

That event took place about fifteen years ago. Just as important to me as saying it was the fact that I was obedient to God in what he asked me to do. It took me a few years, but I finally did it.

Telling my dad I loved him, was a part of resolving a significant issue in my life or at least bring some closure. I knew that for me to become emotionally healthy, I needed to forgive my father for not being there for me as a kid and young adult. Even though my behavior was part of the problem, like I said earlier, I feel like the fact that he was the parent should have caused him to try harder.

I can honestly say, though, that I'd forgiven him for that a long time ago—several years before our exchange in the mall that day. But I also felt lead by the Spirit to tell my dad that I loved him so that the issue would be put entirely to rest.

Let's close by showing how these attitudes were working out in my life through the journey to tell my father I loved him.

Attitude of Truth – Truth was I did love my dad, and he loved me. The truth was we both had a difficult time to say it. The truth was I felt I needed to say it to bring closure.

Attitude of Love – Because of God's love for me, I have learned to love all people. Again, I did love my dad, and as hard as it was, I finally told him. I love my kids greatly and dearly and needed to be an example by telling my father, their Papa, that I love him.

Attitude of Grace – Well, I have received God's grace that I bountifully live out daily. Because of His grace, I am empowered to show grace to all people. There is not one ounce of unforgiveness in my heart toward anyone. What great peace and joy this brings to my life.

I carried bitterness and anger toward my father for leaving my mom and me for many years. When I forgave him, an enormous weight was lifted off of me. When I told him I loved him, it was a way of acknowledging forgiveness between the two of us.

Attitude of Gratitude – I am thankful for countless things in life. I am truly blessed. I am thankful for the many years my kids and I got to travel from California to Missouri for our annual family reunion to spend time with my dad and the rest of my family.

Attitude of Humility – I live my life with the mindset that "I am as good as the best but no better than the rest." I am genuinely humbled by the love and grace of God, our loving Father. I choose to humble myself daily. I consistently pray for God to keep me humble. If I had not humbled myself those years ago, I would not have been able to tell my father I loved him.

Attitude of Acceptance – I learned a long time ago to accept people for who they are but not allow their bad behavior to drag me down. An attitude of acceptance has brought great peace to my relationships with all people.

I have also learned to accept whatever life brings my way. Both good and bad. "It is what it is." It was vital for me to understand and accept my father without judgment. To accept the fact that my father was who he was. He was not a man to express his love through words. When it comes to these types of emotions, he did not show them. By accepting him for who he was, I was able to let go of certain expectations. It empowered me to forgive him. And, eventually, tell him I loved him.

Attitude of Perseverance – I, like many others, have had plenty of challenges throughout my life. I am so thankful that I have not given up. There are things I struggle with now. I know I will persevere! I persevered and eventually told my father I loved him. As a result of my perseverance, not just in this event, but many things throughout life, I am a better person for it, and I am truly blessed.

Neither my father nor I had said "I love you" since that day until he had a stroke in September of 2018, I did tell him a few times while he was in the hospital. I don't think he was coherent enough to hear it. He passed away without ever hearing me say it again. Knowing we've both said it those years ago was better than never saying it all. I am thankful I was present during his passing.

> "For this very reason, make every effort to add to your faith goodness; and to goodness, knowledge; and to knowledge, self-control; and to self-control, perseverance; and to perseverance, godliness; and to godliness, mutual affection; and to mutual affection, love." **2 Peter 1:5-7**

As cliché as this is—life is short. That is a simple truth. Another truth is, life is messy and full of conflict. I assure you that if you can adopt these attitudes and choose to incorporate them into your personal narrative and live them out daily—**YOUR LIFE WILL BE BETTER!!**

> "The great thing to remember is that though our feelings come and go God's love for us does not."**— C.S. Lewis**

I used John 3:16, Luke 10:27, 1 Thessalonians 5:1, and 1st Corinthians 13:4-7 to create a love creed to live by. It encompasses all seven attitudes. This is the core of my personal narrative. I reworded it a bit to provoke a more personal connection to its meaning. I choose to do my very best to live by it.

This creed—this mindset, helps me keep things in proper perspective, God's perspective. I hope you will benefit from this in the same way I have. Having love at the core of your personal narrative will significantly better your life and those around you.

If ever there was a formula to live by to have a peaceful and abundant life. This would be it. Learn it! Live by it!!

Love Creed

In accordance with God's word.

By Stephen Ross

Jesus loved me enough to die for me, even though I didn't deserve it. Therefore…

I will Love the Lord my God with all my heart, soul, strength, and mind. I will love myself and love all people as myself.

I will seek and extend forgiveness to others when needed. I will do my very best to encourage others and build them up.

I will be patient and kind. I will not envy, boast, or be proud. I will not dishonor others, I will not be self-seeking, I will not easily anger, and I will keep no record of wrongs. I will not delight in evil, but I will rejoice with the truth. I will always seek to protect others. I will always trust in God, always hope, and always persevere.

By doing this…

<u>I WILL NEVER FAIL</u>.

Dear Reader,

Thank you for reading Coactive Attitudes – 7 Attitudes that will Change Your Life.

I hope that you get the most out of embracing these attitudes and living them out in your life. They have been life-changing for me and continue to be extremely beneficial in my life.

Coactive Attitudes is an excerpt from my book Coactive Living. If you want to go deeper and learn more about a coactive narrative, coactive mind, and coactive process, please check out my book Coactive Living. It will be available soon.

The following pages are a vision of the wellness ministry I am praying and hoping to build. I have a deep desire to help people overcome their issues and complete their goals. Specifically, as it relates to healthy living in the following three dimensions of wellness—Relationship (God, self, and others), Health (physical, spiritual, and mental), and Finance (budget, debt, savings).

Please pray that God will give me wisdom, put the right people in my path, and provide the resources needed. It's a hefty goal, but we will see where the Lord leads. At this stage—it's just a dream that's starting off with a book.

Be blessed….

Stephen Ross – The author and founder of Coactive Living.

If you would like to get involved or contribute to getting the following ministry up and running, please contact me at:

stephenross@coactiveliving.com

or call 831-277-0867

Also, contact me if you would like more information

Personal Wellness

Relational – Health – Financial

We teach, equip, and coach individuals to coact with God, self, others, and life to overcome and achieve

www.coactiveliving.com

Welcome

Welcome to Coactive Living!

We are glad that you are inquiring about Coactive Living. If you are trying to lose weight, get fit, enhance your relationships, get your finances in order, or make any other changes in your life, then we would be honored to assist you.

All our coaches have been trained and equipped to design a customized action plan to meet your specific needs. The program takes a holistic approach and deals with three dimensions of wellness; relationship, health, and finance.

Coactive Living books, workbooks, videos, and website www.coactiveliving.com will provide you with resources to help you overcome issues and achieve your goals. It will also help our coaches better assist you.

Thank you for checking us out.

About

Coactive Living is designed to equip individuals to make positive and practical changes in all aspects of life. We provide one on one coaching, small group support, interactive website, community resources and networking, videos, and printed resources such as Coactive Living book and workbooks.

Coactive Living teaches and coaches individuals to coact (work together with) God, self, others, and life. We use a combination of - Biblical principles, Narrative Therapy, CBT (Cognitive Behavioral Therapy), DBT (Dialectical Behavioral Therapy), and ACT (Acceptance Commitment Therapy).

Simply put – individuals will be taught to discover what they believe about specific issues in life that they want to overcome and specific goals they want to achieve. They will then learn to accept and embrace them and seek truth within them. Then coact with that truth to help bring forth the changes they desire.

Philosophy

Too many times, people want to make changes in their lives, whether it is finances, relationships, health, or just life in general, only to find that the process becomes more of a burden than the issue they want to change. Often it is because the issue becomes a battle or even a war. At Coactive Living, we take a holistic approach to the individual's lifestyle, equipping them with tools and resources to overcome issues they may face as well as the issues at hand.

We realize that there is a dialectical exchange (conflict) between our creator and us, within ourselves, with others, and life (our circumstances). This understanding helps us search for the truth and reason our way to a healthy personal narrative and behavioral patterns. We then teach and coach individuals to coact with this understanding by embracing and letting go of their struggles. Also embracing their weaknesses as well as their strengths to learn and grow from them.

We believe that all aspects of our lives function within three dimensions of wellness—Relationships, Health, and Finance. The Coactive Living model will help shift a person's way of thinking (personal narrative) to achieve a healthy and fulfilling lifestyle in all three dimensions of life.

Purpose

- Implementing Coactive Living Wellness in churches, businesses, and other community centers.
- Place individuals in a coaching program to help them navigate through the Coactive Living program.
- Conduct relevant speaking engagements, seminars, and workshops for the community.
- Assess individual needs by using Coactive Living methods to help design an individualized course of action. Then we provide encouragement, tools, and resources to accomplish each client's unique goals.
- Educate individuals to take a coactive approach to life by applying the coactive principles conveyed in the Coactive Living book, workbooks, seminar guide, and video sessions.
- Partner with individuals to help solve a wide range of problems utilizing community resources as needed.
- Train and equip individuals to identify opportunities to coach others effectively.

Mission Statement

We teach, equip, and coach individuals to coact with God, self, others, and life to overcome their issues and achieve their goals.

Wellness

We focus on three dimensions of wellness; relationships, health, and finance. With Christ being at the center and encompassed by the spirit of God. We must understand the impact that each of these dimensions has on one another.

Coactive Approach to Relationships

Creates healthy relationships with **God, self, and others** through love, forgiveness, understanding, and communication.

Coactive Approach to Health

Creates a healthy **physical, mental, and spiritual** being through proper nutrition, consistent exercise, and healthy thinking patterns.

Coactive Approach to Finances

Creates an understanding of **budgeting, debt, and savings,** which leads to fiscal responsibility and healthy financial behaviors.

Three Dimensions of Wellness

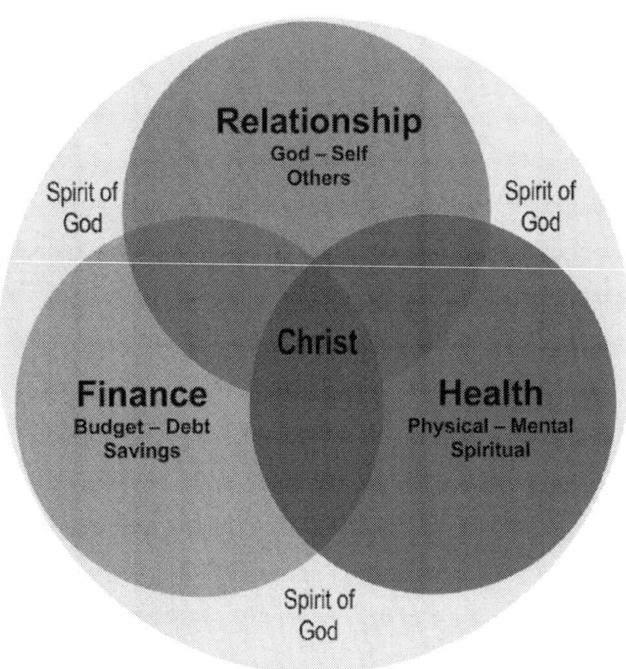

Coactive Living Model

We have designed an effective Coactive Living model (based on principles found in scripture and practiced in the field of psychology) that will facilitate clients and their coaches to develop a customized action plan according to the client's specific needs to help them be successful in overcoming their issues and achieving their goals.

Service We Offer

Faith-Based Coaching:

Weight loss – Spiritual - Finance – Credit – Career – Marriage – Relationship – Divorce – Circumstantial – Parenting – Social – Time Management – and more

Workshops and Seminars:

Individuals, Couples, Church, and Cooperate

Fitness – Nutritional – Time Management – Healthy Marriages – Singleness – Dating – Mate Selection – Healthy Parenting – Single Parenting – Financial Stability – Organizing Skills – Customer Service – Sales – Business Operations – Custom

Training:

Coaches – Small Group Leaders – Small Group Facilitators

Coaching

All our coaches are ICCA certified. ICCA International Christian Coaches Association is a subsidiary of the AACC American Association of Christian Counselors.

All our coaches are trained and qualified to use the Coactive Living model effectively. Our coaches are empathetic to the needs of our clients because many of our coaches were previous clients and have successfully gone through the Coactive Living program.

Two pathways to become a coach:

Already meet the standards of wellness in the three dimensions of wellness. Complete Coactive Living coaches training, and complete ICCA certification. Complete the Coactive Living program. Complete Coactive Living coaches training, and complete ICCA certification.

Our goal is to train coaches and small group leaders in churches and other organizations to lead small groups and coach others in their organization using the coactive living model and program as well as a variety of other resources.

Prison Ministry Program:

Offer coach training to inmates along with free books and workbooks

Addiction Program:

Offer coach training to addicts along with free books and workbooks

Products

Books

Coactive Attitudes – 7 Attitudes that will Change Your Life

Coactive Living – Overcome and Achieve

Take this Cup – Overcoming Fear and Anxiety

Love Creed – Formula to a Content Life

Children's Book Series – Adventures of Zion and Zigzag
(Coactive Living and Coactive Attitude for kids)

Workbooks and Small Group Studies:

Coactive Living Seminar Guide

Coactive Living Workbook

Coactive Health Workbook

Coactive Finance Workbook

Coactive Marriage Workbook

Coactive Singles Workbook

Coactive Parenting Workbook

Coactive Peace Workbook
(Overcoming Fear and Anxiety)

Self-Development Tools:

Financial Software

Daily Planner

Time Management Software

Organizing Skills Development

Interactive Website

Coactive Living APP

Links, DVDs, and Audio CDs:

Variety of Self Development Titles

Inspirational Speeches

Videos

Apparel and Gifts:

T-Shirts with Coactive Living Quotes

Other Gifts with Coactive Living Quotes

Interactive Website

Personal Profile - Post Pictures – Post Blogs – Build Social and Team Network – Direct Access to Message Coach – Customized Profile Builder

Coactive Kids – Educational Games, Activities, and Wellness Tools

Each Dimension of Wellness will have individual:

Bible Studies eBooks and Articles

Developmental Tools

Personal Assessment Test

Resource Links

Commonly Asked Q&A

Relationship

Resources and tools to help enhance your relationship with **God, self, and others**.

Marriage Resources, Tools, and Networking

Parenting Resources, Tools, and Networking

Singles Resources, Tools, and Networking

Relationship Builder (Marriage, Parenting, and Dating)

Relationship Personality Test

Compatibility Test

Communication Assessments Tools

Coactive Kids

Spiritual Gifts Assessments

Online Bible and Study Tools

Videos

Health

Resources and tools to assist in **physical, mental, and emotional** health.

Personality Test and Assessment

IQ Test and Assessment

EQ Test and Assessment

Mental Health Assessment and Tools

Stress Management Assessment and Tools

Mental Health Professional Finder

BMI (Body Mass Index) Calculator

RMR (Resting Metabolic Rate) Calculator

Fitness Plan Developer

Nutrition Plan Developer

Worksheets and Forms

Videos

Financial

Resources and tools for **budgeting, debt, and savings.**

Financial Assessment

Interest Calculator

Debt Reduction/Elimination Calculator

Debt Tools and Forms

Credit Report Access

Credit Repair Resources and Tools

Budgeting Tools and Forms

Videos

Twelve Week Program

We offer a twelve-week program which provides one on one coaching, small group support, workshops and seminars, and interactive website resources for relationship enhancement, weight loss and management, financial management (credit repair and debt reduction), and lifestyle changes.

Our primary objective is to coach our clients to obtain and maintain permanent lifestyle changes. This can result in a 12 to 30-pound loss of weight during the program and continue to lose or maintain weight after the program until our clients obtain a healthy weight.

During the twelve weeks, our coaches will also implement a financial, debt, and credit building process. This will include budgeting, spending, saving, debt reduction/elimination principles, and creditor negotiations.

Our coaches will coach our clients in other areas of life to be determined by the coach and the client. We offer coaching for relationships, divorce, singles, social, circumstantial, career, time management, and several other areas. We will provide information on a variety of resources throughout the community to help solve a wide range of problems and achieve goals.

We also have in house social events and resources. This, along with networking community events and social activities, will provide our clients with healthy and vibrant social opportunities and networking opportunities.

If you would like to get involved or contribute to getting Coactive Living ministry up and running, please contact me at:

stephenross@coactiveliving.com

or call 831-277-0867

Also, contact me if you would like more information

Made in the USA
Middletown, DE
22 September 2022